Credit: karan sidhu

"

For my Mother
Sukey - bringer of
joy, light, humour
and above all, fun.
xx

Modern South Asian Kitchen

Recipes and Stories Celebrating Culture and Community

Sabrina Gidda

Photography by Maria Bell

Hardie Grant

QUADRILLE

contents

introduction

This book is a celebration of South Asian stories, people and food. It looks at the journey of a Punjabi girl who became a chef in London, after leaving her hometown of Wolverhampton. It is one story of immigration, acclimatization, adjustment, flourishing and celebration. It looks back at where I came from and where I may go. It is a snapshot of a new culture that sits between two others. Except it doesn't sit anywhere – it dances freely around, evolving constantly and will continue to do so for some time to come.

This book is about creating new traditions as well as honouring old. It's about being proud of who you are and who you want to become. This is food that is playful, inclusive and fun.

I grew up accessorizing heavily (from a very young age) with my sunglasses – and either a fish finger clenched in my little fist or a chicken drumstick. Some may argue this is a habit I have not grown out of; I might be inclined to agree. I have always been as happy eating eggs and waffles as I am in my ultimate Punjabi eating mode (I once ate 6 bhature with chole and I wasn't even 11). We looked forward to our English Sunday roasts that were as regular on our tables as dhals and rotis; we enjoyed lasagnes, burgers, traybakes and cakes. My parents managed to bridge our cultures and we were raised to enjoy everything – and to make sure we tried everything. Developing a fussy eating habit was a luxury we were not afforded.

Growing up, my eating was varied, diverse and exciting. It reflected a progressed stage of settling in the UK that my parents had successfully managed. And now I am looking at how I can bridge some of those traditions with the world in which I live in. In this quest to find modern ways to connect with my culture I wanted to create a collection of recipes that use similar ingredients. You won't need to keep buying items every time you make a dish – a little investment in your cupboards will allow you to use the recipes in any number of combinations. More of this in Kitchen Pyar (see pages 28–31).

The more I speak to chefs and friends from all backgrounds about the foods they most adore, the more I find that people struggle to recollect course 6 of 18 on a tasting menu. Instead, they are reaching back to food that comforts them and brings them happiness. With these dishes come memories of people – of those they are lucky enough to still have and those who may no longer be with us – but food and thought fills us with gratitude for the time we had together.

This book is for anyone who loves food, loves cooking, loves people. It is one I hope my South Asian friends will enjoy cooking from. I also hope people of all cultures will find things that resonate with them – and that they enjoy the food! And I hope it opens doors as well as conversations. And allows you to be proud and cook and enjoy your food in a new space without the pressure of making it exactly how your relative made it. It is, after much cooking, talking and pondering, wonderful if you can make something exactly the same – but also totally OK if you can't.

Make time to cook with your elders as it is a priceless opportunity to connect in a very special way. Cook for them, show them what you can make, and share it with them. I promise that even the most fierce of bibis will appreciate you making the effort – and if she doesn't, that's OK too: you can't please all of the people all of the time!

Losing my mum meant I had to stop. Not just pause, but stop. And then make sure I had remembered all she had taught me. Life happens and sometimes you take for granted the abundant knowledge and skill that is around you, until one day you don't have it any more – and that, my friend, is when you need it most.

There are very many of my Punjabi peers who don't feel comfortable cooking 'apne khanna' – 'our food' or the food from our culture, and I want to say I hear you. The first few times I cooked dhal it was totally nerve-wracking – so much deliciousness to live up to?! Even now my rotis aren't round but I hope you know it doesn't matter. The fact that you made them is what matters – or that you made your dhal, then had it with frozen Shana chapatti – it's fine to be melding a little day-to-day convenience with it all. I think there should be a little less judgement and a lot more encouragement.

All the little additions, the special ways you choose to do things in your family, making something the way you all like, is absolutely 110% what this book stands for. I hope these recipes will help create fun bases from which you can evolve your own ideas, and allow you to play, and create new exciting food memories for yourselves moving forward. I am totally rooting for you.

This is food that is playful, inclusive and fun.

the new normal

Historically, when I have cooked for my family there have been occasions where this sense of 'other' has arrived and been mentioned in my food. It isn't quite like anything we have eaten before, but it's 'still Indian'. It is with this acknowledgement, acceptance and pride that it is an honour to be able to cook the classic dishes of my heritage, but also dance around in the playful area that sits between those dishes and the classical techniques used in my professional career.

For me it is important to recognize more than just the dish. We must recognize the spices, the journey, the people, the story of our food – and consistently pay homage and tribute to it. This won't always be by making food the 'traditional way' – it will involve being creative and playful, whilst staying connected to my culture.

There is a particular kind of truth in what people refer to as *cucina povera*, literally 'poor cooking' in Italian, with a heady irony in how delicious and rich in meaning the food often is. By 'truth' I mean it is a perfect snapshot of real life, real cultures and real experiences of those who are cooking. The term spans people, countries, continents: it is a universally magical way of cooking. When travelling through Italy and France on more than one occasion I saw nonnas and mamas cutting vegetables in exactly the same way I have seen the women in my family do it. No chopping boards and big chef knives, but a small sharp paring knife, cutting against their thumbs and often straight into the pot – surely a sign of having more in common than difference.

I have come to realize that I'm now in the middle of my life and have experienced first hand the traditional food of my ancestral heritage but am now cooking in a new world, a new time of life – and I feel I have a responsibility to honour both. There are legacies, traditions and deeper meanings to food that I want to make sure I carry forward, but I also want the freedom to cook in a way that is influenced by my experiences. I am someone who sits solidly on the foundation of what came before me but I am also looking to the future with excitement.

Classic French, Italian and Far Eastern travels have been eye-opening opportunities to experience new disciplines and techniques. I have been lucky enough to enjoy some remarkable restaurants across the world, but my most memorable dining experiences have always been those unassuming places, run by families without pomp and often without accolade. Perhaps more than this, is that I am in the process of becoming one of those people that I look up to! So what traditions will be important to me, for my family moving forward? And which dishes will be met with excitement and enjoyment from the next generation?

Authenticity. What is it? Does it mean we only have to cook in the way we have only ever known? Or does it mean standing between cultures, between generations, between our history and our future – and then, just cooking. Enjoying, creating, celebrating, storytelling. By default what we create (if done often enough) will become tradition, and in time, will have its own stories and then eventually become legacy.

South Asian food need not be difficult to make, time-consuming, unhealthy, a 'treat meal' or something you only eat when you visit home. I think we should be engaging all of the time. Some of my peers cook traditionally perhaps once a week, maybe once every two weeks – often in a batch cook (I love a batch cook!). But many have said that it feels like a big work up – or that when they cook South Asian food, it is often only classical dishes they have had passed down to them.

Many of my friends from other backgrounds eat out at Indian restaurants frequently and associate the meal with being big, heavy, hearty, spicy and, while thoroughly enjoyable, not something they would necessarily cook at home. The perception is that it may be too difficult, take too long or require such an inordinate number of ingredients that it's easier to eat out.

I talk about 'kitchen pyar' a lot. It means love for your cupboards and it's not just a romantic notion – by sticking to the list, you can cook the recipes in this book with just these dry ingredients. They will rescue you in times of need, provide an abundance of fun and flavour, and enable you to play with your food!

It feels right to cook in a way that acknowledges all I have learnt from those around me, from my travels and of course the ingredients I love. I also feel that this is part of a wider narrative of life experience, not just immigration in the classic sense but the movement of people globally to experience different cultures and cuisines. The respectful acknowledgement of where we have been inspired, who has inspired us and who we may, in turn, inspire in the future.

"

Creating new traditions as well as honouring old.

a love letter to Dudley Road

"

I was born and raised in Wolverhampton. I am tremendously proud of this and I want to take a moment to tell you about Dudley Road. For as long as I can remember, this road has been home to all kinds of deliciousness. Since I was a very young child my family came here to purchase all the different kinds of vegetables, sometimes meat from the butcher and, of course, the wholesale-sized bags of lentils, atta and spices that we would get through, not as a small restaurant operation, but as a home.

Dudley Road is where you go if you need thoof (incense), floral garlands, pooja trays, diva for Diwali, colours for Holi, gifts for Ramadan, lightbulbs, taps, wholesale retail items, eggless cakes, saris and salwars, bindis, or you want your car valeting, an MOT, a light snack, a big dinner, 3 kilos of jalebis to take to your friend's house for a celebration. It has it all.

My brother and I would walk around with my parents, eyes and mouths agog at how much choice there was. How many kinds of dhal? How many different whole spices, dried spices, oils, flours? I thought roti was roti? And then the achaar aisle… Accustomed to eating achaar from Nimbu in Lambra (usually smuggled in among plenty of clothing on a British Airways flight from Amritsar), I could not believe the pickling possibilities and choices on offer.

I was taught by my mother which day was the best day to go for fresh items, which day the meat arrived from the butcher, and what times of day to shop to avoid waiting at the tills. This often was before or after school – or early morning on a weekend before most of the town had woken up. Mum taught me how to select the nicest chillies and what to look for in the vegetables, I will always remember her picking up a piece of ginger, and snapping off a small nub to make sure it wasn't too fibrous. A habit I have adopted wholeheartedly ever since.

Dudley Road has evolved and of those early-day shopkeepers, some have come and gone, some are new, some have expanded their operations as a mark of their success – and it is really joyous to see. This brings me to the food. When I was a student returning home on a usually awful train from Euston to Wolverhampton, my mum would ask my dad to leave 30 minutes early to collect me, so that he could bring a freshly fried samosa and a paneer roll from Lakshmi. After the always arduous journey of those then-Pendolino trains, it took a minute to stop swaying as I got off the train to find the car, my dad and my samosa. There are times in life that will never be forgotten – but

love really is bringing a hot samosa to someone after a schlep of a journey. What a welcome home.

Let's talk about purchasing – which is never in even numbers. So perhaps you have four guests for tea; you would never, EVER go to Lakshmi and order four samosas and four paneer rolls. Lunacy. You would order at least five of each (Punjabis there were five Pyare, five Ks) and then, just before committing to your order, this would be followed with: 'Let's make it seven of each, plus 2 kilos of jalebi and some ladoo.' Purchasing a finished product by kilo weight is something that I have only really seen in South Asian stores and I can't tell you how much I love it. It is the ultimate signifier of generosity and hospitality – and so indicative of how welcoming our cultures are. These items were revered up and down the country – and it wasn't uncommon for a few kilos of jalebis, mathri and a few dozen samosas to be ordered before a very long drive up north to see family.

It has provided me with a warm welcome on many a return from London – plus a hefty and consistent dose of snacks – and without it I would not have been able to source all of the ingredients needed to create the recipes for this book.

So, whether you're getting yourself some delicious bhindi from Uppal's, samosas from Lakshmi, idli and oothappam from Dosa Hut, a Desi pizza from Mr Singh's, or mithai from Barfia – I can promise you Dudley Road has exactly what you need. Or at least, what you didn't know you needed until I told you about it.

what is it we look for in food?

Whenever I would return to my family home after running various restaurants with modern European food, I was always met with something tremendously special – food cooked by my mother Sukey. I have always been fiercely protective of the food I enjoyed at home. For me, it wasn't 'like' anything else, it was personal, and I looked forward to an email from my mum asking for 'menu requests'. I would respond – often after she had finished cooking – and she would chuckle at getting 5/5 right on my request, matching the delicious things she had made.

Sukey Gidda to me has always been a remarkable woman. A rule-breaker, game-changer, get-it-done type of woman. She was glamorous, loved to dance, couldn't tell a joke before laughing at the punchline, an incredible cook, golfer and sportswoman. She was a teacher for 27 years, a leader, a light – and a bringer of joy and fun to our family. She is all I can ever hope to be.

Cooking and my craft has been a consistent anchor for me. Rain or shine, good times, dark times – cooking and food have helped me. I read a Bee Wilson article in which she quoted food writer Laurie Colwin who observed: 'No one who cooks, cooks alone.' Having done a trilogy of *Great British Menu* I think I could contest this – but it is true.

Truthfully, it explains acutely what food and cooking has meant to me. Initially in my lightbulb moment, it meant I discovered a natural ability. Then I realized that this could be a career for myself at a time when it wasn't really the done thing. For as long as I can remember, cooking for myself and for those around me has given me an incredible sense of purpose and joy. To prep, to cook, to sit down and eat, to feed others is often romanticized – and often equally the exact opposite in a professional capacity. But feeding people is the ultimate joy.

What it does do is connect you to people. Cooking has led me to national competitions like the Roux Scholarship, to television and, in turn, the opportunity to write this book. It has enabled people to see me from afar and ask: 'Are you Mrs Gidda's daughter?' or 'Where are your glasses from?' It is visibility, perhaps hope and, with some luck, inspiration.

I would have found it impossible to write this book without sharing the climate in which it was written. I am forever grateful that I was able to share news of this book with my mother at a time where good news was so sparse for us as a family. I spent a last summer with her in the kitchen, where she used absolutely all the remaining energy she had to cook her dishes with not just me, but us. Never for a second could I allow myself to acknowledge that this was it, the last time we would ever cook together, so I just kept on keeping on, peeling, chopping, listening and learning while being a bit upset about her using so much energy to cook. For her it was imperative that she show us, that we listen, that we learn – and that we remember.

Throughout my time looking after my mum, I was a full-time chef to her. Eating and stage 4 pancreatic cancer don't go hand in hand with ease. And good days filled us all with tremendous hope while bad days were full of the darkest despair. It was a time where all my life skills I had learnt were being put to use. I made juices, salads, mashed potatoes, custard, cakes, scrambled eggs – trying to operate as fast as I could to make sure I could deliver what she felt like eating before the various waves of chemo took away her appetite. It was a new learning experience of balancing medication, side-effects and, of course, the way her cancer made her feel. She never once complained and she will remain the bravest woman I know.

So, even now when I think of all we cooked – cauliflower cheese parathas, lamb chops, her chicken curry, the biggest trifle you have ever seen – she was supervising us to cook food she was physically unable to eat. She knew, throughout the lifetimes of all of those around her, how much we loved her food and how bereft we would all be without her. I cannot manage thinking about how desperately sad it makes me to know we will never cook together again, or hear her taste something I have cooked and tell me 'that's a bit good'. It is a life-altering sucker punch that greets me multiple times of the day, multiple days of the week.

Waking up every day for five months to cook for my mother, to look after her, to play Scrabble while she was having chemo gave me a tremendous sense of purpose. It transcended all other purposes or needs or wishes. Every moment of every day was about making sure Mum was fed, hydrated, looked after, loved and not in pain. Losing her meant for a little moment I lost that purpose too.

I have spent more time than ever at my family home in Wolverhampton with my father as we learn to enjoy life again (strict orders from Mrs G). Initially we leant into the kindness and love of our family delivering food to us – or some of those amazing places on Dudley Road. But very quickly I found myself wanting to go shopping, get the vegetables and start cooking, not how I cook, but how Mum cooked. It became so important to me that, despite the sheer unfathomable weight of grief, I couldn't and never wanted to let it jeopardize retaining what Mum had shown me. I began to make dhal, pakoras, baby baingan sabzi with kalonji, saag pork – all at home, our family home. In her kitchen. With her pots, pans and spoons. And here it is, where Laurie Colwin's observation becomes apparent, that we never really cook alone. I wanted to make everything in the exact way and would ask my father and brother if it tasted right. By 'right' I meant 'like Mum's'. The answer to which we all know the answer: nothing

can ever be quite the same, but as Mum would say 'delicious darling'.

It has become a new purpose for me – to be able to teach these recipes to my niece Amaira. The bond she shared with my mother was remarkable, and I feel clearly a baton handed to me by my mother to make sure that Amaira knows and loves all the dishes my mum would have been making for her in her years to come. So really, it's not the food, it's the message isn't it? The dish is trifle except it isn't: it is so much more. It is my mum's playful, light-hearted, joyous nature – perfectly summarized in a dish she loved to make, for those she loved, and loved to eat. There is a game-changing magnitude to those 'family dishes' that were once a delicious everyday part of life but now carry so much more than just flavour – they are a legacy of love.

a love letter to Tooting High Street

"

Tooting High Street gave to me a particular kind of comfort. It was my Dudley Road in south London. The two may be over 130 miles apart but still neighbours in community, spirit, deliciousness and abundance of choice. Even now the only thing that worries me about moving out of London is: where will I buy fresh curry leaves from at 10pm? – that, and: what would I ever do without being 7 minutes away from Lahore Karahi's kebab naan roll?

On moving to the area, I began the slow and steady process of visiting each establishment to lock in my 'dish'. I tried to find kheer as good as mamiji's (the closest I got was probably Spice Village), and found chicken karahi from Lahore Karahi, and thalis at Jaffna House. On homesick days as a student I would pop into the sweet centre and ask for one jalebi. This would immediately be followed with a bag being placed on a scale and someone loading in a whole kilo of jalebis. When I interjected and requested one jalebi I was greeted with the warmest smile, a warm jalebi and being told 'koi bat nahi' – meaning 'it's OK, no problem' – and being gifted my jalebi for free. It seemed mad to them to charge for one little jalebi, and mad to me that this warmth and kindness I had known in my community was to be found here, in London of all places.

Much like its Wolverhampton counterpart, Tooting High Street has the same eclectic collection of shops, so apart from being a road full of deliciousness, here you can purchase headscarves, sim cards, have your nails done, find bangles of every possible colour known to woman, get yourself a gold chain or do your dry cleaning. There's also the absolute joy of Tooting Market – food vendors next to textile retailers, art shops, bubble tea and wooden statues – it's remarkable. It also helped me see that there is space in London for everyone. It isn't without its difficulties and challenges but the least we can do to support our communities is to shop with them.

The high street has changed greatly over the last dozen or so years, with the arrival of many new food operators and offers, resulting in a very cool food scene. It is a rather magnificent mix of old and new cultures and communities and it remains somewhere I love to be. It gives me retrospective access to Wolverhampton, to Soho Road in Birmingham and it repeatedly grounds me in the rich and wonderful memories of my earlier years. If you have not been to Lahore Karahi for a kebab naan roll, I implore you to stop whatever you are doing and go – there cannot be anything more delicious at this price point available in south London.

I shop at Bhavin's for dry goods, at Daily Fresh Foods for the most amazingly fresh veg and I can, hand on heart, say that there has never been a time where I have come to shop and not purchased a cheeky samosa, a box of chaat or a little parantha as my 'car snack'. Pooja Sweets for chaat, Ambala for gulab jammun, Dosa n Chutney, Namak Mandi for Afghani kebabs and a naan the size of a parking space. It is an amazing, rich celebration of why I love London. And not the boujee Mayfair London, or the sterility of the square mile London, or the cool hipster Shoreditch London – though they are wonderful – but the kind of London that is home to many different cultures, all with chairs pulled up to the high street tables, doing some very delicious things.

For those with more delicate sensibilities, the raucous riot of activity to be found on Tooting High Street might feel a little overwhelming. At which point I would say, probably best you stay at home – unless you roll up your sleeves, get stuck in and jostle about, otherwise you will most certainly miss all of the fun.

sisters – stories & suppers

When writing this book, for a moment I was concerned about whether or not this story had been told. And then I realized that it had and it hadn't. Have there been stories told of South Asian immigrants settling here, all over the country – working through decades of challenges within their own communities and those in which they settled? Yes. Have they eloquently discussed the impact their food has had on their journey – and what it has meant to them? Yes. Does this mean that we shouldn't keep sharing our stories? Absolutely not.

There is something really remarkable when your story resonates with others. When you can provide an opportunity for even a part of a story to be seen or heard – and that for me is what this book is about. Growing up in the 90s, I rarely saw anyone who looked like me on the television, let alone cooking on the television. The only person who I even slightly managed to connect to was Madhur Jaffrey (legend) and an occasional regional news reporter.

So how can we be what we can't see? Visibility is something that I feel very strongly about. At school I was lucky enough to be accepted for who I was (which in all fairness was probably a pared-back Punjabi who fitted in well) – but not a proactive celebration of who I really was, culturally or religiously. There was no study of my culture or history at school – and therefore I assumed it wasn't necessarily that important to know about it. Except it was, and it is. Our knowledge of our history – familial, cultural and historical – came from being at home, with our elders around the dining table. Therefore our histories are all incredibly personal to us, because often we don't get to share them or discuss them with anyone outside of our culture and this, I think, is a missed opportunity for understanding and also to acknowledge generations' worth of achievements.

Stories of partition, what families had to do to survive, to manage, to thrive – it was all first-hand delivery, not from a textbook in a classroom, but by those who lived it. My paternal Biji would speak of her childhood, life with her father in the army – a doctor in the world wars – and how she came to the UK with my grandfather and how difficult it was to settle. Some stories would be hard to tell, a type of gut-wrenching sadness at not just what they witnessed, but what damage was caused to their homeland and what could have been avoided. And some full of joy, fondness and smiles at times gone by, or particular moments when family came together and there was remarkable joy and many tears of happiness.

These are our stories – present – and ready to be uncovered, and they are stories told with the language of food. This is not just the story of one culture but of many cultures and the ultimate wider movement of remarkable South Asian immigrant women. Grit, graft (some of the original multitasking mothers, often helping juggle not just their own families, but also leaning in to help their sisters along too), sacrifice, hardship, love, celebration – these women have experienced it all. It is impossible not to acknowledge our entrepreneurial, brave and beloved elders who left much behind and in doing so created a new opportunity for themselves and their families. (A collection of once-in-a-generation experiences, so full of power, love, sadness and opportunity that truly we can only pretend to understand.) It was at home where I first witnessed the skill and knowledge of South Asian cookery, from women in kitchens – experts at their craft, willing and ready to pass on their knowledge to the next generation.

When my grandmother arrived in the UK, it was 1960. She was in Wolverhampton, and was running a house like clockwork, looking after not only

her family, but managing a swift rotation of shift-working Punjabi settlers needing an interim home while they saved to become permanent residents with their own homes. She would pool vouchers for condensed milk, milk powder and sugar with other households and make barfi, an Indian sweet for them all to share. She found ways to replicate and mimic ingredients that were not yet readily available – to create a type of cooking that would be familiar enough for everyone to feel at home, despite being so far away.

When my grandfather became a publican it was my biji who would be upstairs with her friends and family, supervising the production of round and flat lamb kebab patties, samosas, aloo tikkis and her version of imli chutney. This chutney was in fact a perfect mix of mint sauce, ketchup and brown sauce. Not traditional by any means – but in 1962 nobody was policing tradition. They wanted to feel as near to home as they could – and these versions of home food helped people feel a little closer. I have to add that it was the sale of these little snacks along with THAT chutney which allowed her to purchase not one, but three houses in the 1960s. Unheard of at that time of life for a woman, let alone a little Punjabi powerhouse called Iqbal Kaur.

With these clever concessions on tradition came the same amount of pride in what was being created. Food wasn't 'less than' because it wasn't an exact replica of the food of the Punjab – it bought the comfort of home, familiarity and gave rise to new traditional dishes that became family favourites for generations to come. My mum would tell me about 'bread rolls' – which were effectively white sliced bread, filled with samosa filling, rolled up, the ends pinched and deep-fried. Found nowhere in the Punjab, but lending a vast amount of joy to those eating them in Wolverhampton at the time!

These are the dishes I want to celebrate. The dishes we don't really find in restaurants, the dishes that tell a story for us, the dishes that are important to our families, the dishes that allowed us to celebrate our food and culture by being different, the dishes that connect new generations back to those before – and the dishes that can, with the same freedom of creation, allow us to create new traditions and classics that we are equally proud of.

Every time I take a moment to think about my family, our friends, extended family and all who sit in our Punjabi infrastructure, I marvel that none of them have ever made a bad meal. Sure I ate food that was sometimes too spicy, or someone served karela (bitter gourds – I still can't abide them to this day) and sometimes the roti might have been a bit thick. But our entire network is united by exemplary skills in the kitchen. From the simplest and most humble of dishes to the most complex – it is something that I took for granted as a child but have immense retrospective gratitude for now as an adult.

There are also important stories to tell of my own culinary cultural journey and narratives I am keen to discuss, so that the next generations of my family will be able to share, celebrate and make their own.

When I began cooking in professional kitchens, I started in the realm of modern European cookery. Gastro pubs, underpinned with classic French technique, The Sanctuary Spa in Covent Garden where I was head chef, and then on to the City at AIG and Freshfields LLP. All of it was led with a modern European viewpoint – not because it was compulsory but perhaps because in all of my formative aspirational years as a chef it signified skill, credibility and professionalism. To some extent I am sure that is correct – and it taught me a collection of remarkable skills and disciplines that have since impacted the way I prepare food in many cuisines, including my approach to Indian food.

Indian home cooking has always signified skill, but I always thought of it as a softer, more flexible, enjoyable way to cook and eat. It was home, family, warmth, comfort and celebration. Indian food feels like hospitality, warmth and generosity to me – and a celebration of a more personal side of me. So what happens when all of these travels, all of this learned experience, life experience, culinary disciplines, history, culture and heritage come together? It is impossible to unlearn all of that experience, so perhaps now the future is a vibrant combination of all of the above.

This book also came with an opportunity to reach out and speak to some remarkable women of South Asian heritage to find out about the dishes that mean something to them, their stories, and what they are doing to hold on to and amplify their cultures. There was no exacting brief, other than sharing and talking about things that mean something to them. Many have started businesses, many are in the next phase of evolution in their culture – one that recognizes the power of immigrant pathways, and the impossibility of not being influenced by all you experience culinarily. The contributions from Usha, Nisha, Rajinder Auntiji, Lakshmi and her friends, Chandani, Mursal and Zohra Aunty, Ruchita and Melissa are gratefully received. Cooking with them was treasured time and I thank them all for welcoming me into their homes to listen, learn and share.

Identity, food, cooking, culture, heritage, history – all of our family stories, all of our journeys – everything, absolutely everything, makes us who we are in life but most generously, how we are in the kitchen. Our cultural history is linear but the life experiences that work around this are varied and when these moments collide, we can create something really quite exciting.

Sacrifice, hardship, love, celebration – these women have experienced it all.

kitchen pyar

Growing up, our cupboards were filled with the usual suspects: ketchup, HP sauce, noodles, once upon a time Smash, baked beans, a tin of spam (which was kept, I think, out of nostalgia by my mum, because I don't remember eating it) and in the freezer were frozen peas, oven chips (French fries) and – most importantly – my favourite, fish fingers. Alongside all these British staples sat a wholesale realm of Punjabi classics: ice-cube trays filled with ginger garlic paste, frozen okra, bags of frozen homemade paneer, cooked tarkas and masalas, gram flours, rice, pulses, lentils and an abundance of spices.

This has always felt natural to me, and to a very large number of South Asian families across the UK, I am sure. A joyous hotchpotch of cultures and cuisines melded together to create a new normal. Not just 'normal' but a space with an opportunity to create something playful and fun, that celebrates all aspects of our palates. In the same way our homemade Asian ingredients were nestled firmly in the freezer next to the chips or peas, we too have always been perfectly comfortable with what this jostling of cultures creates.

For many of us, our cupboards start off with the best intentions – organized, labelled, stacked in an easy-to-find way – and quickly become an incidental storage spot for ingredients we purchased to cook with once, then relegated to the back of the cupboard because we haven't made the dish again. Speaking with friends (and from experience) there is a good collection of recipes here that allow you to use up some of the spices you'll find you already have but also some great items I would encourage you to purchase to save time, and give you the ability to bring something together quickly and without a huge lift.

I freeze as much as I can whenever I have a little surplus, no matter how small the portion, and with a sense of karmic culinary reward it helps me to make something out of almost nothing. For example, half a portion of dhal I had frozen came out to be mixed with some onion, curry leaves, a pouch of rice, finished with crispy shallot and lemon and it was a fast-fix khichdi. Sometimes we need to be able to deliver – and to do so quickly! This level of thrift and adeptness to create is not new. It takes us all the way back to the highly skilled family cooking that has been generationally honed, with just a few modern shortcuts.

Sometimes your kitchen can become a place full of slower-paced contributions: chutneys, pickles, jams, slow-cooked curries, stews, spice blends and meals that may take a little longer to prepare. We might have items that were made for us, food given by family and friends, to be enjoyed whenever the time came that we need it most. My mum's kitchen has always been abundant with this pyar – given with blessings and love – and it still very much is. The freezer is laden with little containers and packets of her home-cooked food and I cannot tell you what it means to me to be able to take something out to eat when I need it most. There is something quite remarkable about the fact that while she is physically no longer with me, she manages to nourish and to love me at the same time, with this food, these spices, these cupboards and this kitchen.

Kitchen pyar – for the love of your kitchen. Fridge, freezer and cupboards all loved up to make sure they love you back when you most need it.

These are the ingredients I would not be without in my kitchen:

SPICES

Amchoor (dried mango powder)

Asafoetida (hing)

Black cardamom

Black pepper

Cassia bark

Cinnamon

Cloves

Coriander seeds, whole and ground

Cumin seeds, whole and ground

Fennel seeds

Fenugreek (kasoori methi)

Green cardamom

Kashmiri chilli powder

Lindi pepper

Mace

Mustard seeds

Nigella seeds (kalonji)

Pomegranate powder (anardana)

Saffron

Turmeric

and a great garam masala

SAUCES, VINEGAR AND OIL

Maggi hot and sweet sauce

Mustard oil

Rice vinegar

Tamarind sauce (imli)

ACHAAR AND PICKLES

Brinjal (aubergine/eggplant) pickle

Chopped green chilli pickle

Green mango pickle

Lemon and ginger pickle

CRUNCHY AND CRISPY THINGS

Crispy dhal

Crispy onions/shallots

Desiccated (shredded) coconut

Dukkah

Nylon sev

Peanuts

Sev

FAST-FIX CORNER

Canned chickpeas (garbanzo beans)

Canned coconut milk

Canned kidney beans/mixed beans

Coconut cream

Gram flour

Microwave rice

Red split lentils

AND IN THE FREEZER

Chilli/ginger/garlic pastes – blitz in a food processor or blender. Remember to remove the skin of the garlic and ginger and destalk the chillies before blitzing. Keep a few whole green chillies in the freezer too – they are great to throw into tarkas for finishing off dhal.

Coriander (cilantro) leaves, stored in a ziplock bag

Fresh curry leaves

Any additional marinades left over from your prep

I like to make sure there are enough of these items in stock – so that no matter how little I seem to have of each, I can create something quickly and without needing to buy too much. I would also encourage you to shop in your local Asian stores. Best of luck with not purchasing more than you went in for, but when you look at the pricing, choice and quality, you won't be disappointed!

Brunch

"

A betwixt-meals
meal, with no
particular start or
end time. A rule-
breaking meal
window designed to
throw you perfectly
off the straight and
narrow. For friends,
for family, for
togetherness,
or just for you.

For as long as I can remember brunch has been a thing in our family. Everyone began the day with an initial breakfast of cereal, and then there was a second meal on a weekend that was designed to tide us all over until pakoras in the afternoon. There is something about this meal window; for some it is all about eggs Benedict, club sandwiches and mimosas. While I love this – and have enjoyed many such a brunch – sincerely my favourite is omelette and paratha, pickle and yoghurt. It has taken me the journey of my 35-year life to eat as much as I have, in as many places as I have, all over the world – to gently but committedly return to where I began. There is something really very special about it.

When I was growing up, everybody played a part in the assembly of brunch. I would lay the table in my earlier years (before I graduated to egg scrambling, then on to my masters in chopping onions), Mum would scramble eggs and Dad would be on onions, fried with green chilli, finished with fresh coriander.

This move was done ahead of schedule, so that we could synchronize production of ajwain parathas (Mum) and omelette (Dad). Someone would have to get the big jar of achaar, then my brother and I would take 10 minutes to pick out the bits we liked – lime and ginger for me, chilli and mango for him. Homemade yoghurt would be put into little bowls, pickle on plates, spoons at the ready… and then the arrival of a stack of parathas and a lovely plateful of folded omelette. Heaven.

So for me, brunch is an important opportunity to break out of the three regular meal windows and have some fun. I do feel that there should still be some ceremony though. This might mean laying the table and eating sharing style, creating something really special or just setting out your weekend papers and cutting your toast in triangles instead of squares. The choice to create your own ceremony is entirely up to you but I invite you to do something for you – it feels wonderful.

These recipes are a mix of the dishes that I loved to eat growing up with some playful versions that for me dance around in the technicolour playground of how I cook. The cauliflower cheese paratha will always be special to me. In an ideal world there would be a few items on the table, plus a pot of masala chai and a gaggle of people picking at and enjoying it all while having a good old catch-up.

One of my favourite dishes as a child in this brunching window, was a Bird's Eye potato waffle, with a fried egg and tarka beans. It is the perfect mash-up of East meets West classics – and I am not sorry about how much love I have for waffles even though these days I make my own. As always, I encourage you to play and in doing so, create your new traditions.

masala tortilla

One of the most important breakfasts of all time for me is masala omelette – the most perfect balance of chilli, onions, spice and fresh coriander (cilantro). I cannot tell you how many times I have made – or indeed eaten – this with ajwain (carom) paratha and homemade yoghurt, with a little achaar. JOY in every way. So for those of you who may not want to stand at the stove making one omelette at a time when you have your friends over for brunch, behold this: the LEGIT-imate love child of a Spanish tortilla and a masala omelette. You can make one, feed everyone at once and use just a little ajwain butter on toast to give you all the classic flavours.

SERVES | 4–6

8 large free-range eggs

2 large white onions, very thinly sliced

Olive oil

2 Indian green chillies, finely chopped

1 tsp garam masala

Generous handful of chopped coriander (cilantro)

30g (1oz) butter

Salt

1 Crack your eggs into a mixing bowl, whisk up and season with salt.

2 Fry your onions in a splash of olive oil in a 20-cm (8-in) non-stick frying pan (skillet) over a medium heat (you can use other types of pan but the stress of sticking isn't worth it for this).

3 Slowly sweat the onions – you can allow them to colour a little as this gives amazing flavour. This should take about 12–15 minutes. Add the finely chopped green chilli, garam masala and a good seasoning of salt.

4 Add your coriander, stir for a moment before adding the butter.

5 Once the butter has melted, add the eggs and gently mix, making sure the onions are well dispersed in the tortilla.

6 Turn the heat down low and cook for about 15 minutes. Now, if you are feeling brave, you can invert the tortilla onto a plate and slide it back into the pan before cooking for a further 15 minutes. Alternatively, if your pan is ovenproof, pop it into the oven for 10 minutes at 180°C fan/200°C/400°F/gas mark 6 until the top is set.

7 Allow the tortilla to rest for 10 minutes before you cut in.

8 Eat with hot ajwain buttered toast, salad or however you please.

gobi brunch muffins

Muffin making – but make it Desi. I love making these, they are so easy and are a really delicious and different bake to bring to the brunch table. You can make them a little spicier and play around with the vegetables, but the key is to keep veg small so that they cook through and don't sink to the bottom of the mix. Finish with the tempered spice for a little extra magic.

MAKES | 12

250g (9oz) self-raising (self-rising)flour

1 tsp baking powder

1 tsp salt

150g (5½oz) crumbled feta

150g (5½oz) cauliflower, broken into small florets

25g (1oz) chopped coriander (cilantro)

1 tsp green finger chilli, chopped

1 heaped tsp ginger paste

1 bunch of spring onions (scallions), peeled, chopped and washed

½ tsp garam masala

¼ tsp ground turmeric

WET INGREDIENTS

2 eggs, beaten

100ml (½ cup) vegetable oil

250ml (1 cup) milk

FOR THE TINS

2 tbsp vegetable oil, for greasing

100g (3½oz) fine semolina (farina)

TEMPERED SPICE

1 tsbp vegetable oil

8 fresh curry leaves

1 tsp black mustard seeds

2 dried hot red chillies

1 Preheat the oven to 200°C fan/220°C/400°F/gas mark 6. Mix all of the muffin ingredients together in a large bowl.

2 Mix the eggs, oil and milk together until well combined in a jug.Carefully pour the wet ingredients into the dry, being sure to mix well.

3 Grease a 12-hole muffin or cupcake tray with the remaining oil. Sprinkle in the semolina before shaking out any excess.

4 Divide the mix evenly in the tray and bake for 20 minutes until a skewer comes out clean. When the muffins are risen, golden and cooked, remove from the oven and allow to cool slightly.

5 In a small saucepan or frying pan (skillet), add all of the tempered spice ingredients and bring to a sizzle over a medium–high heat.

6 Using a spoon, pour the tempered spice over your muffins and serve.

green chilli cheese croque

Green chilli and Cheddar are absolutely glorious together. If you add a little fresh coriander and a bit of onion, then you get the magic. This is a speedy version of a very classic French dish, Croque Monsieur – I love it. I also love the fact that this is vegetarian and, frankly, it is a reliable fix should you be feeling a bit delicate after a rather wonderful evening partying. Add a little jaggery bacon (see page 51) if you have any left or keep it totally veggie – up to you!

SERVES | 2

2 Indian green chillies, finely sliced or chopped

1 small red onion, finely sliced or chopped

200g (7oz) grated (shredded) mature Cheddar cheese

3 tbsp chopped fresh coriander (cilantro)

2 ripe tomatoes, seeds removed and flesh diced

1 tsp garam masala

4 slices of white bread (can be a country loaf)

Pinch of salt and a few twists of black pepper

Oil, for frying

COATING

3 large free-range eggs

3 tbsp milk

Pinch of salt

Pinch of Kashmiri chilli powder

½ tsp garam masala

1 In a bowl, mix the chillies, onion, Cheddar, coriander, tomatoes, garam masala, salt and pepper.

2 Divide the mix between two slices of bread and top with the other slices to make sandwiches.

3 Press the sandwiches down at the sides so the filling doesn't fall out.

4 Beat together the ingredients for the coating in a shallow bowl. Dip the sandwiches into the egg mix, turning to coat both sides.

5 Heat a little oil in a non-stick frying pan (skillet) over a low heat. Pan-fry each sandwich for 4–5 minutes on each side, turning as you go.

6 Serve with Maggi hot and sweet sauce and topped with a fried egg, if you like, to make a Croque Madame.

onion bhaji babka

This is a tremendously celebratory dish. It takes a little time and effort to make, but it's so worth it. I can't think of anything more glorious than a warm spiced onion bread and here it is! You can add a bit of extra Parmesan to your onion mix if you fancy a little more richness. I tend to make this in a 900g (2lb) loaf tin (pan) or a round cake tin (pan).

MAKES | 1 LOAF

FILLING

Oil, for sautéing

2 good-sized white onions, finely sliced

1 tsp green chilli paste

1 tsp garlic paste

1 tsp ginger paste

¼ tsp ground turmeric

½ tsp toasted and lightly crushed coriander seeds

½ tsp cumin seeds

½ tsp salt

2 tbsp chopped coriander (cilantro) stalk

1 tsp ajwain (carom) seeds

2 tbsp grated (shredded) Parmesan cheese, optional

1 First make the filling. Heat the oil in a pan and sauté the onions, chilli, ginger and garlic pastes over a medium heat for about 15 minutes or until soft and a little golden. Add the turmeric, coriander and cumin seeds, salt and coriander stalks. Remove from the heat and add the ajwain seeds and Parmesan if you like. Set aside to cool.

2 For the dough (see ingredients overleaf), put the flour into the bowl of a mixer fitted with a dough hook, add the sugar at 12 o'clock, the salt at 4 o'clock and the yeast at 8 o'clock.

3 Make a little well, add the eggs and milk and mix for 4–5 minutes. Increase the speed and add the butter a tablespoon at a time – only adding more when it is well mixed.

4 Add the nigella seeds and mix on a medium speed for 8–10 minutes until the dough leaves the sides of the bowl and becomes smooth and shiny.

5 Flour your work surface with the mix of sifted gram flour and semolina. Roll your dough into a rectangle – much easier when the longest side is closest to you – about 1cm (½in) thick.

6 Scatter over your onion mix evenly. Then roll up the dough, Swiss roll fashion and mix as you would a Swiss roll from the top to the bottom. Cut the dough lengthways through the middle.

7 Turn each length cut-side up, so that the filling ingredients are facing up. Pinch the two lengths together at the top and then begin to braid them by lifting one over the other – pinch at the bottom to seal.

Continued overleaf

onion bhaji babka *continued*

DOUGH

275g (9¾oz) plain (all-purpose) flour

25g (1oz) caster (superfine) sugar

½ tsp salt

5g (⅛oz) fast-action dried yeast

2 eggs, beaten

50ml (scant ¼ cup) whole milk, at room temperature

80g (2¾oz) unsalted butter, cubed and softened

1 heaped tsp nigella seeds (kalonji)

ROLLING & FINISHING

2 tbsp gram flour

2 tbsp fine semolina (farina)

Soft butter, for greasing the pan

8 Brush your tin (pan) lightly with a little softened butter and a sprinkle of any leftover semolina/flour mix on your work surface.

9 Lift the braid into the tin. If you do this one side at a time, you can tuck each end under so you are left with a lovely open braided onion mix on show.

10 Cover with a clean tea towel (dish towel) and prove at room temperature for about 2 hours or until it has doubled in size.

11 Towards the end of the proving time preheat the oven to 190°C fan/210°C/410°F/gas mark 6½. Bake the bread for 15 minutes, then reduce the temperature to 170°C fan/150°C/300°F/gas mark 2 and bake for 35 minutes or until a skewer comes out clean.

12 Allow to rest for 15 minutes and then turn out onto a wire rack. Serve with any of the spiced butters on page 182.

Dad's proper porridge

For most of my life the only place I have eaten porridge (oatmeal) is at home. Why? Because once you have eaten porridge like this everything else feels a little less delicious! Porridge, or dalia, is almost dessert-like in its richness and frankly it sets you up until dinner time. In our household this dish is made by my dad, and my goodness he does it brilliantly. Since I was a baby I have been eating this and I love the fact that even now it signifies weekends, relaxation, comfort and us being together. It also starts with a sizeable chunk of butter, which can only be a good thing! I couldn't make porridge any other way now.

SERVES | 4 (WITH SECONDS)

80g (2¾oz) salted butter

220g (7¾oz) rolled Scotch porridge oats (oatmeal)

4 green cardamom pods

3 cloves

900ml (scant 4 cups) whole milk

Sugar or fresh fruit, if you like

1 Pop your butter into a large saucepan over a medium heat, allow the butter to melt and start to sizzle before adding your oats.

2 Add your oats, stirring constantly, to toast them until your kitchen smells like granola – then add the cardamom and cloves.

3 Pour in the milk, stirring constantly, and bring to the boil before reducing the heat to low and letting the porridge simmer. This should take about 15–20 minutes and it will begin to thicken. As the porridge cools it will thicken further, so don't over-reduce it.

4 Top with a sprinkle of brown sugar or fruit and enjoy.

Cauliflower cheese paratha

I am lucky enough to be able to say that my beautiful mother had a remarkable repertoire of extremely delicious dishes and these certainly became iconic for us. Mum first tried these when they were made by my father's aunt (Chachiji, who was also known for her legendary lemon and ginger achaar) – and from this point, my mother was hooked, and so in turn, were we! Mum loved to make these for our family – because she knew how much we love to eat them. It's also a testament to Chachiji's remarkable cooking that these have become such a favourite in our household. There was no advance preparation time here: Mum would roll, assemble, cook and send out servings one by one to us – and in turn we would be able to have our hot paratha, sometimes sharing in halves if we had greedily already eaten ours, always eaten with homemade yoghurt. Then the time would come when we would have already eaten two each and be sharing the last one, and Mum would join to have her paratha with us – I will always remember her asking, 'Is it ok?'. She knew – it was faultless and flawless (as always) and made with so much love.

MAKES | 6

DOUGH

500g (1lb 2oz) medium wholemeal atta (chapatti flour, which is not the same as regular wholemeal or wholewheat flour), plus extra for rolling

1 tsp salt

4 tbsp vegetable oil, plus extra for cooking

350ml (1½ cups) lukewarm water

FILLING

1 small cauliflower, trimmed and cut into florets

3 tsp fresh ginger, finely chopped

2 Indian green chillies, chopped

½ tsp salt

¾ tsp garam masala

Handful of grated (shredded) mature Cheddar cheese

¼ tsp ajwain (carom) seeds

½ tsp cumin seeds

1 To make the dough, put the flour and salt into a good-sized bowl. Add the oil to the water and slowly add to the bowl as you work the dough by hand (or use a mixer with a dough hook on slow speed). As this dough has no yeast we don't want to overwork it, just until it is smooth and even.

2 Cover the bowl and allow to rest for 1 hour at room temperature.

3 Meanwhile, make the filling. Mum would pop all the ingredients into the processor and pulse until coarse and even. You want a crumb, not so fine that it loses texture, but not so chunky that it will break free from the dough. (If you don't have a food processor, grate (shred) the cauliflower, then mix with the remaining ingredients.)

4 Tip into a bowl ready for the paratha making and divide your rested dough into 12 even-sized balls.

5 Take your first ball of dough, dip into a little flour and roll into a disc about 7cm (2¾in) in diameter. Take another ball and roll it to about 8cm (3¼in) diameter. Put a generous spoonful of filling in the centre of the smaller disc, and then pop the slightly larger one over the top, stretching to seal the mixture inside. The key is to not over-flour, so the discs stick together. Repeat to make 6 parathas.

6 Then carefully flour your work surface and dip each paratha into some flour. Begin to roll each paratha to create an even round circles – about 16cm (6¼in) in diameter.

7 Cook on a tawa or flat cast-iron pan for 5–6 minutes, turning from time to time. Brush one side with a little oil and cook face down on the tawa for colour. Serve with fresh plain yoghurt and pickle, if you like.

Biskut Bar
Chandani Kohli

I first heard about Biskut Bar when Chandani asked to do a cook along with me during lockdown. Biskut Bar is her brainchild and is a marketplace of aromatically bold, premium contempory Indian biscuits and snacks. Chandani develops each recipe with ethically sourced ingredients. I received a tin of the most delicious biscuits that had a way of being comfortingly familiar but also modern, with playful illustrations, all sustainably packaged. (Being planet positive is an important part of the Biskut Bar ethos.) It was like being served up a little plate of my own culture in a way I hadn't known before, supremely cool and very delicious. Aside from the usual suspects served with tea, the mass-produced and nostalgic biscuits I had always known, I hadn't really experienced an artisanal biscuit that celebrated my culture in this way.

Born in Chandigargh, Chandani was raised in Virginia via the UK, 'a right of passage' en route to the US she says, and one travelled by a few of my own family members. Chandani's father is a doctor and her mother very well educated and very well travelled, so a new life in the US beckoned. It involved just the nucleus of their family going to a place without a well-established community of South Asians and no doubt it was an exciting, nerve-wracking and life-changing move to help establish the next phase of family life and opportunity.

Chandani's mother grew up in Japan. Business took her maternal grandfather to Japan where he initially exported Japanese auto parts to India, then Japanese fabrics to the UK and today exports Japanese auto parts around the world. He also built the first Gurdwara in Kobe, Japan. In turn her mother speaks Japanese as a first language, followed by Punjabi and English. It seems that her mother had the 'third-culture kid' experience, with a clear Japanese influence featuring prominently in her upbringing and most certainly on the table. Chandani says that she feels like the next incarnation of the third-culture kid, experiencing for herself much of the Japanese culture through her mother, along with being in the US, and also having a connection to Punjab and now living in London.

She is blessed with the mantra, 'Food is sustenance, nourishment, pleasure and comfort' and it comes with some really open, refreshingly honest conversation about motherhood, cooking, setting up a business and how many hats there are to wear! Being in her kitchen, drinking chai and cooking is a joyous moment of 'real talk' and I love her frankness. For her, like so many of us, the language of food is how we are able to pass on our cultural heritage, our stories and our identity to the next generation, something Chandani is consciously doing with her own children. She turned to her mother to learn more about traditional Punjabi cooking and unsurprisingly encountered that moment so many of us have. Recipes are not in books, cooking times and temperatures are not definitive and quantities of ingredients are done by eye, by hand and just by knowing. It leaves us all there to absorb (seemingly by osmosis) generations upon generations of skill and knowledge to help us continue the eternal joy of family cooking.

"

Food is an identity.

> " Food is sustenance, nourishment, pleasure and comfort.

We cook panjiri together, a North Indian Ayurvedic nutritional supplement as it were. This lady doesn't just make biscuits, you know! If you have never had panjiri before, you must try it. It is eaten through winter to help the immune system and also given to new mothers to promote healing, lactation and energy levels. It is utterly delicious. I remember when my niece was born, my grandmother and mother got together to make panjiri for my sister-in-law – it is such a wonderful act of love between women. Naturally I am overjoyed that we get to cook this together in Chandani's home while she tells me all about her remarkable life and her business. There are so many ingredients in panjiri and she is very exacting about the quality of those that she uses. We begin with homemade ghee and the toasting of gram flour as the heat works through the pan. I am transported to various moments cooking with my mum, my grandma, being in India – all sorts of familiar sensory alarms are being set off. This is really what she means about connecting people with their culture through food. As a self-professed 'city girl' she also told me how choosing to 'make something traditional, from agricultural regions of Punjab helps me to connect to my culture in a different way' and, as we speak of my imminent trip to my ancestral village in India, this strikes a chord with me.

So what is it like for her children, now second-generation, third-culture kids, and how can she keep them aware of their cultural identity? Chandani makes a point of celebrating traditional Indian holidays not just the Western ones her kids may be used to. She uses this as an opportunity to share with them the significance of festivals such as Diwali, Bandi Chhor Divas and Vaisakhi, but the most effective way to connect them to their culture is 'on the table'. Her mother cooked Indian food but also Japanese food, so it was 'not uncommon to see a Japanese-style pork fried rice being cooked, and a pan of chai on to boil at the same time', which is probably a perfect

image to show the side by side embracing of all of the cultures she is able to enjoy.

She acknowledges the skill and the wonder of traditional home cooking, learnt by eye, but she is also happy operating in a progressive, pragmatic way when she cooks. Another dose of 'real', which is refreshing. As an entrepreneurial mother, running a business, I really wanted to know what she loved to cook when she was in 'home mode'. She used to make multiple dishes when cooking at home, a couple of sabjis and dhal, but life doesn't always allow that. So now when cooking dhal, she adds additional sabji vegetables into the dhal as a way to tackle both dishes in one. 'Our food is so multidimensional – and so exciting, so it can be really daunting to get it right in the way that it is traditionally made. But now I love to cook in my own way, freely and without rules.' Smart move. Parathas are a free-for-all for any sabji she has made and often break out of the classic aloo, mooli and methi versions and may be filled with aloo gajar (carrot and potato) or any number of creative sabjis. I like this approach, and her declaration that she likes her 'food to work for me and for us as a family. I am not about "authenticity" in that sense. Because of the nature of my upbringing, I both honour my heritage and recreate the inheritance in a way that is authentic to myself: a little off the cuff.'

We sit down to eat biscuits and, of course, panjiri, along with plentiful amounts of chai. Chandani is infectiously passionate about wanting people to know about Indian biscuits and be excited about them. She believes in 'accessible, enjoyable Ayurvedic cooking' that isn't just for South Asian people. This is food for everyone. People have embraced ashwagandha, chai and turmeric lattes, and she's right that it's time to have utterly delicious Indian biscuits to sit alongside those things. Chandani's ethos for her business is 'all-American curiosity, rooted in the Punjab, baked under the British sun' – a remarkable celebration of her third-culture magic.

masala eggs, yoghurt, feta & tempered spice

It's just not brunch for me without eggs. I absolutely love them. This is a version of an iconic Turkish eggs dish I have eaten many times over the years. You can make this with soft-boiled eggs too if you wanted to serve it as part of a sharing brunch. It is a great way to make sure you keep using up your spices by bringing them forward into your meals!

SERVES | 2

Splash of white vinegar, for egg poaching

4 free-range eggs, as fresh as possible

½ tsp Kashmiri chilli powder

250g (9oz) Greek-style yoghurt, at room temperature

2 tsp garlic paste

120g (4¼oz) butter

6 fresh curry leaves

2 Indian green chillies, finely chopped

½ tsp cumin seeds

½ tsp coriander seeds

½ tsp ground turmeric

1 tsp ginger paste

100g (3½oz) feta cheese

Sea salt flakes and black pepper

Fresh coriander (cilantro) leaves, to garnish

1 Bring a small pan of water to the boil, add the vinegar and then crack in your fresh eggs. Simmer over a low heat for 3–4 minutes. (If your eggs aren't so fresh, I would recommend frying them sunny side up and finishing the dish in the same way. Equally delicious, I promise.)

2 Meanwhile, stir the Kashmiri chilli powder into the yoghurt along with 1 teaspoon of the garlic paste. Spread thickly over the middle of a serving plate or your bowls if portioning.

3 In a second small pan, add the butter, curry leaves, chillies, cumin seeds, turmeric, ginger and the remaining garlic pastes. Heat to a gentle sizzle until you hear the curry leaves frazzling, then gently swirl until the butter begins to foam.

4 Carefully drain the eggs, pop them onto the yoghurt before pouring over the tempered spice butter. Finish with a generous mill of black pepper and salt, crumble over the feta and scatter over the coriander leaves to garnish.

jaggery & fennel bacon butty

This isn't a swift dish but it is remarkably delicious, and you can make it a couple of days ahead if you are entertaining. I have always championed the life-affirming power of a bacon butty – the first thing we would request when we came home from our travels in India: crispy smoked bacon in bread, plenty of butter and a bit of HP sauce. This is more of a grown-up version: the best way to serve it is with toasted buttered rolls and a panful of fried eggs. It also makes excellent toasties, should you have any left.

MAKES | 4

500g (1lb 2oz) sliced pork belly

1 tsp Kashmiri chilli powder

½ tsp smoked paprika

½ tsp black pepper

25g (1oz) jaggery, grated (shredded)

2 tbsp tamarind sauce

150ml (scant ⅔ cup) water

BRINE

500ml (2 cups) cold water

3 tbsp fennel seeds

1 tsp chilli (red pepper) flakes

35g (1¼oz) salt

35g (1¼oz) sugar

2 tsp coriander seeds

1 tsp garlic powder

1 You will need to brine your pork belly for at least 24 hours before making this, if not 48. Bring the measured water to a simmer in a large saucepan, before adding the fennel seeds, chilli flakes, salt and sugar. Stir until dissolved, turn off the heat and allow to cool.

2 When the brine has cooled, pour over the pork belly slices and leave covered in the fridge (in a non-metallic dish) for 24–48 hours.

3 When you are ready to cook, remove the pork belly slices from the brine – you can do this by pouring it through a strainer. Preheat the oven to 150°C fan/170°C/300°F/gas mark 2.

4 In a bowl, mix together the chilli powder, paprika, black pepper, jaggery and tamarind sauce. Use the mixture to coat the pork belly slices before putting into an ovenproof dish.

5 Add the measured water and cover the dish with foil. Cook for 2 hours until soft. For the final 15 minutes, remove the foil and turn the temperature up to 200°C fan/220°C/400°F/gas mark 6 to caramelize the pork.

6 You can eat the pork with fried eggs, or shred it with a fork before putting into soft rolls.

breakfast sooji

I know lots of people who have nightmares about school semolina pudding. I am sorry if your experience of this amazing ingredient hasn't been remarkable. However, it's fast, super-delicious and very good for you. So, here is my shot at redemption for you…

I make this by totally omitting the sugar because my papa is diabetic, so we are super-mindful of copious amounts of unnecessary sugar in just about everything. Here I have kept the sugar light, but you really can learn to love it without! For a vegan version, swap the tablespoon of ghee for coconut oil, and the milk for a non-dairy alternative. Depending on how loose you want the pudding, just add a splash more milk. Use a whisk for this if you have one.

SERVES | 4

1 tbsp ghee or coconut oil

100g (3½oz) fine semolina (farina)

2 tbsp desiccated (shredded) coconut

¼ tsp ground cardamom

1 tbsp golden caster (superfine) sugar

450ml (2 cups) milk or non-dairy alternative

Cashew or almond nut butter, honey or dark chocolate chips, to serve

1 Heat the ghee in a shallow pan, add the semolina and coconut and whisk over a medium heat to toast. After about 5–7 minutes you should be able to smell a gorgeous nutty, buttery aroma – and certainly see the mixture get a little darker.

2 Add the cardamom and sugar, then the milk, half at a time, being careful that it does not splash when you add it. Keep whisking – the semolina will thicken within about 2–3 minutes. The mixture should be thick enough to eat with a spoon. I top mine with a spoonful of nut butter, and a little teaspoonful of set honey. I also highly recommend dark chocolate chips.

spicy sausage scrambled eggs with tarka beans

This is tremendously nostalgic for me. We often had tarka beans when I was growing up and even now I think this is my favourite way to eat baked beans. Nothing here really takes too much effort yet it is outrageously delicious – perfect alongside a stack of hot buttered toast. If you're veggie, omit the sausage or use your preferred plant-based alternative.

SERVES | 2–4

TARKA BEANS

1 tbsp ghee or vegetable oil

¼ tsp cumin seeds

1 onion, chopped

1–2 Indian green chillies, sliced or chopped

½ tsp garlic paste

1 tsp ginger paste

400g (14oz) can baked beans

¼ tsp ground turmeric

½ tsp garam masala

½ tsp salt

Fresh coriander (cilantro) leaves, chopped

SCRAMBLED EGGS

4 free-range eggs

2 tbsp milk

½ tsp chopped Indian green chilli

½ tsp salt

Pinch of garam masala

30g (1oz) butter

2 Cumberland sausages, skins removed

1 To make the beans, heat the ghee in a saucepan. Add the cumin seeds and, when they sizzle, add the onion. Cook, stirring, for 5–10 minutes over a medium–high heat.

2 Add the chilli, garlic and ginger and cook for 5 minutes or so. Add the beans, turmeric, garam masala, salt and 50ml (scant ¼ cup) water. Bring to the boil, then turn down the heat. Finish with chopped coriander.

3 Meanwhile, beat together the eggs, milk, chilli, salt and garam masala. Melt the butter in a non-stick frying pan (skillet), add the sausage meat and fry until golden. You don't need to break it into crumbs, just fry it until it is cooked.

4 When the sausage meat is golden and cooked through, add the egg mix and scramble to your liking.

5 Pile onto hot toast with the beans alongside.

aloo waffle

Bird's Eye potato waffles, fried eggs and tarka beans = winning on every front. Initially, as a child, my palate was weighted heavily in favour of ketchup, until I firmly stood in camp HP. In this recipe I have opted for a sweet and tangy tomato relish that unites the best of both. You can make this in pancake format if you don't have a waffle iron but I wanted to create maximum nostalgia.

SERVES | 4

400g (14oz) mashed potato

Finely sliced spring onion (scallion)

1 heaped tsp ginger paste

½ tsp garlic paste

½ tsp chopped Indian green chilli

Generous pinch of chopped coriander (cilantro) – use the delicious stalks

½ tsp salt

½ tsp garam masala

2 free-range eggs

2 tbsp grated (shredded) Parmesan cheese

75g (2½oz) plain (all-purpose) flour

Butter or oil, for greasing a waffle iron or pan

Kasundi tomato relish (see page 175), to serve

1 Put the mashed potato and spring onion in a bowl, and add the ginger and garlic pastes, chilli, coriander, salt and garam masala. Mix well.

2 In a separate bowl, whisk up the eggs with a fork until well mixed before adding to the potato mix along with the Parmesan.

3 Sift in the flour and mix again to make sure there are no lumps.

4 Preheat a waffle iron or a frying pan (skillet), then grease or lightly oil.

5 Pop 2 large spoonfuls into the middle of the waffle iron, close and cook for about 5–7 minutes until golden and hot through. If using a pan, cook until small bubbles appear on the surface, then flip and cook the other side for a couple of minutes. Repeat for the other 3 waffles.

6 Serve with kasundi tomato relish and/or a fried egg.

jalebi pancakes, Alphonso mango & pistachio

Jalebi joy! I must say jalebi are a little too sweet for me these days – but I love the idea of them. These pancakes (crêpes) have all the elements of jalebi flavour, but are not deep-fried, and have a little less sugar too! I have paired them with a nice little salad of fresh Alphonso mango and some beautiful pistachios. The slight saltiness of the pistachios works really nicely to balance the sweetness. Now, if you are making these and fancy getting a little bit playful, you can pop the mix into a squeezy bottle and make them look like jalebis – but that is entirely up to you. Kids love them!

SERVES | 2

190g (6¾oz) plain (all-purpose) flour

2 tsp gram flour

1 tbsp caster (superfine) sugar

1 tbsp baking powder

¼ tsp salt

295ml (1¼ cups) lukewarm milk or dairy-free alternative

1 large egg

4 tbsp unsalted butter, melted, plus extra for frying

1 teaspoon vanilla extract

SYRUP

6 tbsp maple syrup

3 saffron strands

½ tsp ground cardamom

1 tsp lemon juice

5 tbsp water

TO SERVE

Sliced cheeks from 1 Alphonso mango

Zest of ½ lime

Crushed pistachios, toasted

1 Mix the flours, sugar, baking powder and salt together in a bowl.

2 Whisk the milk, egg, melted butter and vanilla together and pour into the dry mix. Mix well but don't overmix.

3 Pop all your syrup ingredients into a small saucepan and heat so that the saffron infuses and small bubbles break at the side of the pan. You don't want the syrup to boil, just bring it up, then take it off the heat and set aside while you make the pancakes (crêpes).

4 Heat a large non-stick frying pan (skillet) over a medium heat, then grease the base with some butter.

5 If you are making regular pancakes, spoon a small ladleful of batter over the hot surface – or do a couple at a time if you have space. When the edges seem to set and small bubbles form across the mix, flip and cook the other side for a couple of minutes. Repeat until all the batter is used, greasing the pan again as needed.

6 If you are making jalebi-style pancakes, simply swirl your mix into little jalebi shapes and cook in the same way.

7 Serve with mango, lime zest, a drizzle of syrup and toasted pistachios.

Snacks, Smalls & Sharing

" Elite-level mini meals for all times of the day. Can be eaten as starters, for sharing with drinks or on their own – all guaranteed to bring joy.

'Small plates' has become a bit of a phenomenon. And our bijis and bibis were at it long before it became a dining concept for the masses. Culturally speaking, you would never have guests (invited or unannounced) and not feed them. We come to one of those funny little cultural dances, which happens a lot. As a host you offer chaa choo – coffee, juice – and sometimes you will be met with, 'Gosh no, don't trouble yourselves' or 'No, no – we just came to see you.' As a child I always looked around and wondered what this hoo-ha was about; naturally I was always up for a glass of Rubicon mango and hardwired to be ready to snack at any given moment, and so wondered why you couldn't just say, 'Yes, please!'

Snacks, biscuits, kebabs, pakoras, chai, paratha, dhal sabji … you name it, if anyone knocked on our door at any given moment there would be within the walls of our home (and of so many homes) a secret abundance of hospitality and deliciousness that would be bestowed upon all those who visited. On more than one occasion we had late-night visits from family friends and before you knew it, a plate of kebabs and fried onions appeared, with chutney and raita. It seemed to appear from nowhere; I never saw them in the fridge, which looked sparse to me! But clearly my mum was prepared – she was known for making magic like this happen. And so the evening would ascend into much laughter, a few drinks and a good old get-together.

Snacking, sharing and eating are an intrinsic part of my personality. I haven't met a snack I don't love – and I certainly don't recall a time when I was able to politely decline something remarkable that came from the kitchen of any South Asian home. My entire childhood is full of memories of various aunties, chachis, bibis and bhuas – brilliant women – creating a sizeable quantity of food from a small kitchen, seemingly without many ingredients.

When it came to cooking pakoras, my mum would heat the oil in her kadai and check it was hot enough by dropping in a bit of the batter. Always with the same yellow-handled slotted spoon that she used for well over 30 years. She bought a little deep-fryer once but soon returned to the trusty kadai and slotted spoon. Then, amidst a little 'natter', a mix here and a sizzle there, out came a delicious stack of crispy goodness. It would be onion pakoras first and fish pakoras last, usually made with cod – light, crunchy and just a little bit spicy – then came a nap.

The following recipes are perfect to have as starters, and to serve with bits on the side,or just on their own, to socialize around. Some are super-quick and others work perfectly made in advance and frozen to have on hand, ready to create your own magic moments when you have surprise guests. And all of them are designed to be big wins for flavour and fun.

crispy curry & lime leaf squid

I don't do a tremendous amount of deep-frying, but if I am taking the time to fry pakoras it makes sense to use the oil to fry up some other delicious treats. Squid is one of those things that lots of people have told me they love to order when eating out but wouldn't necessarily buy to cook at home. It's not so tricky – you can ask your fishmonger to do the prep for you, so that when you get it home you just need to wash and portion. It really is very simple. Growing up, we never ate squid but when we were old enough to select our own food on restaurant menus we got a little braver with our choices. This dish is where the fritto misto of my Bernardi's restaurant days meets Punjabi pakoras.

SERVES | 2 GREEDILY

2 large, cleaned squid

50ml (scant ¼ cup) milk

Vegetable oil, for deep-frying

DREDGE

200g (7oz) plain (all-purpose) flour

2 tbsp Kashmiri chilli powder

1 tsp ground black pepper

1 tsp amchoor (dried mango powder)

1 tsp ajwain (carom) seeds

4 curry leaves, finely shredded

2 large makrut lime leaves, finely chopped or shredded

1 tsp salt

TO SERVE

Lemon wedges

Achaari mayo (see page 176)

1 Put everything for the dredge in a bowl, mix well, then set aside ready for the squid.

2 Cut your cleaned squid tube lengthways in half along the natural seam. You should have a sheet of squid. Cut this in half again lengthways. Now, gently score the squid on the angle, making sure you do not cut through the flesh. Repeat the scoring in the opposite way so you have a nice crosshatch effect. Cut the squid into small pieces by slicing across the width.

3 Dip the squid pieces into the milk before coating them in the flour dredge. Heat the oil until a small cube of bread browns in 30 seconds. Fry the squid pieces, in batches if necessary, for about 2 minutes until golden. Drain on paper towels and serve immediately with a wedge of lemon and achaari mayo.

triple fish kebab

There is absolute joy in something being so simple and tasting so great – I really love this kebab recipe. If you want to mince everything you can but I like seeing the texture of the fish within the mix. These can be popped onto skewers, rolled into balls, pressed into patties or shaped into burgers. The point here is that you can do as you please once you are comfortable with how to make this mix. Much lighter than meat, super-fast to make and utterly delicious.

SERVES | 4

200g (7oz) salmon fillet, skinned and pin boned

200g (7oz) cod fillet, skinned and pin boned

1 tsp minced Indian green chilli

1½ tsp ginger paste

2 fresh curry leaves

1 makrut lime leaf

½ tsp salt

½ tsp amchoor (dried mango powder)

1 free-range egg

4 spring onions (scallions), chopped as small as you can and washed

400g (14oz) raw king prawns (jumbo shrimp), peeled and deveined

1 tsp garam masala

60g (2¼oz) white sesame seeds

Lemon wedges, to serve

1 Cut each of your fish portions in half. Keep the nicer bits and pieces for the dice and put the tails or anything else into the food processor. Add the chilli, ginger paste, curry leaves, lime leaf, salt, amchoor, egg and spring onions. Blitz well and turn out into a bowl. Dice the rest of the fish and the prawns into small (5mm/¼in) cubes. I know this is a faff, but if you have time I recommend it.

2 Add the diced fish and prawns to the mix, along with the garam masala and mix well. You can now shape them into 8–10 even-sized patties, burgers or onto metal skewers like koftas. I like to make small burger-shaped tikkis. Sprinkle with the sesame seeds and pop them onto a lightly oiled baking tray and cook under a hot grill (broiler) for 15 minutes, turning halfway through.

3 Serve with lemon wedges.

crispy corn tikki

There is something very addictive about the sweetness of corn with chilli heat. These are a really tasty vegan snack and can be wrapped up like a falafel. Also, you don't have to deep-fry them so you can make them midweek without a massive lift. They also work nicely as little pancakes or crêpes – highly recommended with chutney and a little salad.

SERVES | 4

Vegetable oil, for pan-frying, optional

200g (7oz) canned sweetcorn, drained

4 spring onions (scallions), chopped

2 tbsp ginger paste

1 tbsp Indian green chilli paste

1 tsp salt

50g (1¾oz) gram flour

40g (1½oz) fine semolina (farina)

Juice of ½ lemon

4 fresh curry leaves, chopped

1 tsp cumin seeds

4 tsp roughly chopped coriander (cilantro)

1 Preheat the oven to 190°C fan/210°C/410°F/gas mark 6½, line a baking tray with baking paper and spray with a little oil. Alternatively, put 3 tablespoons of oil into a frying pan (skillet).

2 Put half the sweetcorn to one side with the chopped spring onion. Pop all the other ingredients into a food processor and pulse until coarsely combined. Tip into a bowl and stir through the remaining corn and spring onion. Carefully place 1 large tablespoon at a time onto your lined baking tray or sheet, evenly spaced, and bake for about 10–12 minutes, turning once. If you are frying, heat the oil in the pan and carefully spoon about 2 tablespoons of the mix into the hot oil – cook about 2–3 at a time. Gently turn over as they get golden, remove from the oil, drain on paper towels and serve hot.

7-spiced fried chicken with achaari mayo

There are so many incarnations of fried chicken – and I don't know any meat-eaters who can resist a little spicy, crunchy chicken! Now, if you don't want to deep-fry or shallow-fry, you don't have to. The chicken can be baked in a hot oven on a tray lined with baking paper and a good old spritz of spray oil for crunch. You can use chicken breast cut into strips or use bone-in chicken, but frankly thighs, bone-out, win for me. Super juicy and less faff.

SERVES | 4

400g (14oz) skinless, boneless chicken thighs, cut into 2–3 pieces

Vegetable oil, for deep-frying

Achaari mayo (see page 176), to serve

MARINADE

200g (7oz) natural (plain) yoghurt

Juice of 1 lemon

2 tbsp tamarind sauce

1 tsp amchoor (dried mango powder)

1 tsp garam masala

DREDGE

150g (5½oz) cornflour (cornstarch)

150g (5½oz) plain (all-purpose) flour

1 heaped tsp ground cumin

1 heaped tsp ground coriander

1 heaped tsp ground black pepper

1 heaped tsp ground fennel

1 heaped tsp fennel seeds

1 heaped tsp ground fenugreek

1 tsp salt

1 Mix the ingredients for the marinade together and pop the chicken into it for 24 hours (at least).

2 When you are ready to cook, you will need to use a little deep-fryer, or a saucepan suitable for shallow-frying. Heat the oil over a medium–low heat; you don't want it super-hot, otherwise the outside will crisp before your chicken has cooked.

3 Mix the ingredients for the dredge.

4 Carefully lift the chicken pieces from the marinade, making sure you shake off any excess yoghurt. Dip the chicken into the dredge, coating each piece well. Shake off any excess flour and then gently lay the meat into the oil. It should immediately start to fry well. Working in batches, gently turn over the pieces so they colour evenly – fry for about 7–9 minutes in total until golden and fully cooked. If you need to make them ahead of time, simply fry them to colour and finish cooking them in the oven at 180°C fan/200°C//400°F/gas mark 6 for 10 minutes until piping hot.

5 Serve with achaari mayo as a dip.

onion pakoras

My mum Sukey was known for her knockout pakoras, another of the iconic dishes she made, in particular her spinach and onion version. She made the batter so thin and so light the pakoras only just held together when they were fried, which, most importantly, meant they were triumphantly crispy. And that's crunchy crispy, not greasy or oily – perfect with masala chai – or, as my wonderful mother would have it, a glass of perfectly chilled champagne.

SERVES | 4

Vegetable oil, for deep-frying

Handful of baby spinach (leaves roughly cut in half)

2 large white onions, finely sliced

Biji's chutney (see page 171), to serve

BATTER

150g (5½oz) gram flour

2 tbsp ginger paste

1 tbsp Indian green chilli paste

1 tsp ajwain (carom) seeds

1 tsp salt

1 tsp Kashmiri chilli powder

1 tsp cumin seeds

1 tsp coriander seeds, roughly broken

4 tsp roughly chopped coriander (cilantro)

120ml (½ cup) cold water

You will need a large saucepan filled a third full of oil or a deep-fryer set to 180°C/350°F.

1 So the aim here is for everything to be nice and cold – and for your onions to be finely sliced. Not so fine that they no longer hold their shape but fine enough to get crispy.

2 In a large bowl, mix the batter ingredients together. You want a nice light batter mix – it may feel thin to you, but I promise this is what you need to have the crisp and the crunch. When you're almost ready, add the spinach and the onions and mix well (I recommend using your hand here so you can really mix it properly).

3 Check your oil is hot enough either by adding a cube of bread and seeing it immediately sizzle, or by using an oil thermometer. Take a small amount of the mix and carefully lower it into the oil using a spoon. Don't overcrowd: you may have space for 3–4 of these pakoras at a time. Use a slotted spoon to gently turn them as they become golden. When they are a lovely golden brown, remove them, draining well before popping onto a couple of sheets of paper towel.

4 Eat them hot. Serve with Biji's chutney. And champagne.

spicy chicken kebabs

Kebabs are always a good idea. I have amazing memories of being in restaurants and seeing these incredible 'sizzler' dishes whizzing past, heaped with delicious tandoori meats. It was an integral part of my formative food experiences as a child – and it still gives me huge joy. Seekh kebabs are often made with lamb but I have used chicken here because it makes for a lighter kebab, perfect for forming into tikki shapes or more traditional skewered kebabs, for cooking on a barbecue.

SERVES | 4

500g (1lb 2oz) 6% fat minced (ground) chicken

1 medium white onion, finely diced

2 tbsp ginger paste

1 heaped tsp green chilli paste

1½ tsp garam masala

2 tsp amchoor (dried mango powder)

1 tsp ground coriander

1 tsp ground cumin

1½ tsp salt

2 small pinches of fresh coriander (cilantro), chopped

50ml (¼ cup) vegetable oil

1 Put the chicken, onion, ginger and chilli pastes into a large bowl. Add all the dried spices, salt and fresh coriander.

2 Oil your hands using a little of the vegetable oil, then divide the mix into 6–8 patties. These will work well on the barbecue or under the grill (broiler).

3 Cook on a preheated barbecue/skillet for about 10–12 minutes.

4 Serve straight off the heat with fresh green chutney, naans and salads.

Modaks & Ganpati
Lakshmi Kulkarni

Visiting Lakshmi just a few days before the Hindu celebration of Ganpati was wonderful. Something that is new to me, Ganpati is the celebration of the birth of Lord Ganesh. His life is believed to represent prosperity, wisdom and good fortune, and I learnt so much over a few hours of cooking with these amazing women. I was so warmly welcomed to join these women around the table, to learn, to have my questions answered and to be encouraged to participate. Lakshmi is a Tamilian married to a Maharashtran and can cook many different cuisines – she is truly excited by food – but there is a particular occasion where she mobilizes her sisterhood and wider community and has been doing so for the last 18 years. We are joined by Lakshmi's mother-in-law, Anjali Auntiji, Shree Auntyji and friends Swapnali and Asawari, all of whom are experts in the making of modak.

'We are a group of 15 women who come together every year for a Ganesh Utsav event. This is our 19th year of doing so and it is very important to us.' I am invited into the pre-preparations of this huge celebration that gathers hundreds of members of the community together. This get-together is a free event, with all food offered as a 'prasad' (a blessing), in celebration of Lord Ganesh. Many donations are made to cover the costs of food and the hiring of halls and spaces, with as many as twenty or so families making a contribution.

Traditional sweetmeats called modaks are made in their hundreds, by hand, to be shared. Around the table I watch Lakshmi and her friends having a natter, each assembling with

dexterity these little parcels of joy. Up until recently the lead supervisor in the kitchen was a 92-year-old lady who liked to make sure production was coming along nicely and make sure everyone was 'behaving'. 'You can't imagine the chatter as we are preparing!' Lakshmi tells me. Anjali Auntiji and Shree Auntyji tell me of the history of modaks, and that traditionally they are made with rice flour and are steamed, but that in order to improve shelf life, and also to be able to produce huge quanitities, a pastry option was created, using semolina, flour and oil, allowing the dough to be fried. I particularly love the ingenuity here, so rather than staying wedded to the traditional methods, there has been evolution, allowing easier production and less waste.

Modaks are pastry dumplings, stuffed with a mixture of coconut (Lord Ganesh's favourite), jaggery, cardamom and sometimes sultanas. Not dissimilar to a momo, they respond best when being handled by experts, but I did give it a go! The dough is shaped into a little ball, rolled out with a wooden rolling pin, filled and then pinched and pleated into a little dumpling. I am informed by Shree Auntyji that foods are are either male or female. Modaks are in fact male, so there must be a female version, in this case, a karanji. This is a little empanada-type shape, with a beautiful run of crimping along one edge. Standing around the table, our production operation is in full swing, as Lakshmi fries off the modaks in batches, carefully draining them as we chat.

The celebration started with 50 people in a small hall and has grown to a following of 350

" We are a group of 15 women who come together every year for a Ganesh Utsav event. This is our 19th year of doing so and it is very important to us.

The atmosphere in a kitchen full of women is electric. All ages, all stages, all welcome to enjoy the making of these treats, while catching up and chatting together.

people, all coming together in Basingstoke to celebrate Lord Ganesh in the community. While the event is mixed, the preparation of modaks is undertaken by a group of women, each with a designated task, to contribute in a tight 4-hour or so prep window the day before the event. Up to 500 modaks are made by hand to be served alongside shrikhand, rotis and pulao. All of the women have apple trees in their gardens, so they collectively harvest their apples and make an apple pickle or achaar to serve, not because this is a historic tradition, but purely because they always have so many apples. 'There is only so much crumble and pie you can eat!' says Lakshmi, and she's right; it's ingenious to use what is available to all and I love the idea of a group harvest before sharing with one another.

This is a really special moment, to be in the kitchen with these women, being invited into their prep for a momentous day. I have never eaten a modak, or cooked one, so to do so with a team of experts sharing stories was real-time wonderment! As we cook, Lakshmi tells me about what a brilliant cook her daughter Aditi is and how she cooks most nights at university. It is impossible not to acknowledge the inherited love of food and cooking amongst these women, and the support and nurture offered to the next generation to continue the traditions. Lakshmi speaks with such pride of the 'foodie' love her family and the wider community have, and I can just imagine the wondrous get-togethers over delicious meals that happen around this kitchen table.

The atmosphere in a kitchen full of women is electric. All ages, all stages, all welcome to enjoy the making of these treats, while catching up and chatting together. As this Ganesh Utsav event has grown in the calendar, it has allowed all members of the community to partake. Lakshmi tells me that everyone is welcome, not just those who follow Hinduism. Over time people have learnt prayers and practices and now there is even an engineer who is the official priest for certain weekend events. Children

are welcomed and encouraged to be involved in any way, helping in the kitchen, colouring, creating posters and clearing up. Young children make posters to encourage people not to be wasteful and to 'take only what you can eat'. It seems like a great opportunity to open young eyes to community and to actively take part in the celebration.

Originally from Mumbai, Lakshmi is passionate about home cooking and about communicating through food. She also has a passion for teaching, which is clearly visible from her infectious enthusiasm. She hates food waste, she loves to cook and most of all she loves to feed. She doesn't eat meat, but learnt to cook it when she arrived in the UK and is happy to cook for other people, with much learning through 'British television'. I laugh hard when she tells me of her love for the late Keith Floyd, something we have in common. I ask about masala dabbas (spice tins) and all of the women unanimously declare that there are 'too many spices to fit into one tin!' And out pour the confessions of cupboards and drawers full of spices, used for various different dishes and, of course, how each home's cooking repertoire is so different. Swapnali and Asawari remark on how exciting it is that for each region there are new ingredients to explore and different methods of cooking, which is why they could never tire of eating or exploring South Asian food.

I have such huge respect for these women, helping to maintain this celebration, year in and year out, for ever-increasing numbers. And long may this continue – the celebration of Lord Ganesh, the celebration of this sisterhood, the coming together of these brilliant women and the sharing of their heritage, not just with each other but as a community. I look forward to coming back to celebrate with them in their 20th year.

curried crab on toast

Crab is another one of those items that I would order from menus in my teenage years as I thought it was very fancy – and very delicious. As an adult, I think both are true! I used to make potted crab in the first pub I worked in and it has always felt like a treat. This is without chilli so you can really taste the sweetness of the crab.

SERVES | 4

1 tbsp vegetable oil

2 fresh curry leaves

3 spring onions (scallions), sliced finely

20g (¾oz) butter

½ tsp ginger paste

½ tsp Kashmiri chilli powder

¼ tsp black mustard seeds

½ tsp ground turmeric

½ tsp salt

Couple of twists of freshly ground black pepper

100g (3½oz) brown crab meat

100g (3½oz) coconut cream

100g (3½oz) white crab meat, picked

Juice of ¼ lemon

A little coriander (cilantro), if you like

Toasted sourdough, ciabatta or crumpets, to serve

1 Pop the vegetable oil into a pan with the curry leaves and bring to a sizzle over a medium heat, being careful not to burn the curry leaves. Add the spring onions, butter, ginger paste, spices, salt and pepper. Cook gently for about 5–8 minutes until the spring onions are soft.

2 At this point, pop in your brown crab meat, stirring well. Increase the heat a little and add the coconut cream, which should thicken nicely.

3 Finish by stirring in the white crab meat and lemon juice. You can let this cook for 3–4 minutes but mix it well to ensure the crab mix gets nice and hot.

4 Spoon over hot buttered sourdough toast, crumpets or even across scrambled eggs.

tomato toast, grilled mackerel & amchoor onions

I can't work out what steals the show here, the crazily ripe tomatoes or the remarkable mackerel. Super-fresh mackerel is worth seeking out because it really is one of the best fish money can buy – make sure it is bright-eyed and shiny. In relation to some other fish, it also remains fairly affordable. This dish couldn't be any simpler but it feels very special.

SERVES | 4

3 large ripe (very important) tomatoes, at room temperature

2 tbsp extra virgin olive oil, plus extra for drizzling

Sea salt flakes

1 tbsp tamarind sauce

2 tbsp vegetable oil

½ tsp garam masala

4 unskinned fresh mackerel fillets, pin boned

4 slices of sourdough

1 garlic clove

5 mint leaves, chopped

2 tbsp chopped coriander (cilantro)

Amchoor onions (see page 184)

Pinch of salt

1 Coarsely grate (shred) your tomatoes into a bowl using a box grater. Add 2 tablespoons of extra virgin olive oil, a pinch of sea salt flakes and the tamarind sauce. Set this aside at room temperature.

2 In a separate bowl, mix the vegetable oil, garam masala and a pinch of salt. Use this to coat the mackerel fillets, making sure the marinade covers the flesh of the fish.

3 Make the amchoor onions by putting the ingredients into a small bowl with a pinch of sea salt flakes. Leave to pickle.

4 When you are ready, toast your bread. Once it has toasted nicely and is still warm, rub the garlic clove across the slices and set aside.

5 Heat the vegetable oil in a non-stick frying pan (skillet) and lie the mackerel skin-side down and cook for a couple of minutes until the skin has begun to blister and the flesh becomes opaque. If you want to turn the fish, do so once to show some heat to the flesh, but don't mess with it.

6 To plate, spread a tablespoon or two of the tomato mixture over the toast. Top each slice with a fillet of chargrilled mackerel.

7 Stir the chopped mint and coriander through the amchoor onions before topping the mackerel with a little of it.

8 Finish with another drizzle of olive oil.

market fish with gunpowder

I absolutely love ceviche. It is so fresh, vibrant and full of texture and flavour. In this instance I have given it a little kick of gunpowder, a spice mix you can buy if you don't want to make it, but it is one of those kitchen pyar items that, if you make a batch just once, it promises to reward you in your most bleak culinary moments at home. The key is the best fresh fish you can buy or, if you can't get fresh fish, this works perfectly well with cooked peeled king prawns (jumbo shrimp) too. Just be sure to give them a good squeeze to lose any excess moisture.

SERVES | 2

240g (9oz) super-fresh fish (cod, tuna, salmon, bass or bream), pin boned

⅓ cucumber, peeled

8 ripe cherry tomatoes, quartered

1 small red onion, finely sliced

Coriander (cilantro), chopped

Pinch of salt

Juice of 1 lime and wedges, to serve

GUNPOWDER

3 tsp sesame seeds

8 fresh curry leaves

1 tsp coriander seeds

1 tsp cumin seeds

½ tsp brown mustard seeds

8 dried whole Kashmiri chillies (mild heat), stalks removed

1 tbsp vegetable oil

60g (2¼oz) dried channa dhal (yellow lentils)

1 tsp sea salt (kosher salt)

¼ tsp ground turmeric

¼ tsp amchoor (dried mango powder)

½ tsp coarsely ground black pepper

1 First prepare the gunpowder. Put the sesame seeds, curry leaves and all the whole spices in a frying pan (skillet). Dry-toast for 4–5 minutes over a medium heat, gently swirling the pan. When the aroma of the spices is released, tip them onto a plate to cool. Dry-toast the chillies in the same pan before adding them to the other spices.

2 Pour the oil into the pan and fry the channa dhal until they begin to turn golden – this should take about 5–7 minutes. Remove from the heat and allow them to cool slightly.

3 Put the channa dhal, toasted spices, salt, turmeric, amchoor and black pepper in a blender and blitz to a semi-coarse powder. Your gunpowder will last in an airtight container for a month or so.

4 To prepare the dish, dice the fish into 1cm (½in) cubes, or thin slices if you prefer. Pop into a clean, cold bowl, and then add the lime juice and a pinch of salt.

5 Quarter the cucumber and remove the seeds before dicing and adding to the fish with the cherry tomatoes, onion, chopped coriander and 1 tablespoon of the gunpowder. If you feel your fish needs a little more, add extra gunpowder and a pinch of salt. This should sit for at least 30 minutes before serving.

6 Garnish with fresh coriander and lime wedges.

spiced pepper hummus, black pudding keema & pickled shallot

I feel this dish may cause some controversy. It's loud, proud and decidedly eclectic, but it's worth the effort. My preferred brand of black pudding for this is Clonakilty: the oatmeal gives a really nice texture and the spice blend is a great base. If black pudding isn't your thing, just increase your preferred meat. Minced (ground) lamb, beef or chopped mushrooms work well with this too.

SERVES | 4

HUMMUS

400g (14oz) can chickpeas (garbanzo beans)

1 jar chargrilled peppers, drained

Juice of 1 large lemon

4 tbsp tahini

1 fat garlic clove

Small handful of fresh chopped coriander (cilantro), plus extra to garnish

6–8 tbsp olive oil

Sea salt

KEEMA

3 tbsp vegetable oil

150g (5½oz) minced (ground) pork

1 medium white onion, finely sliced

100g (3½oz) black pudding/morcilla, crumbled

1 tsp Indian green chilli paste

1 tsp garlic paste

1 tsp ginger paste

½ tsp cumin seeds

¼ tsp Kashmiri chilli powder

1 tsp garam masala

Sea salt (kosher salt)

Toasted sesame seeds, to garnish

Amchoor onions (see page 184)

1 Drain the chickpeas but retain the water. Remove any seeds from the chargrilled peppers, pop them into a blender with the chickpeas, lemon juice, a generous pinch of salt, the tahini, garlic and fresh coriander. Blend well, adding the olive oil gradually while blending. If you feel you need a little more liquid, add enough of the chickpea water to give a relatively smooth creamy texture. Set aside while you make the keema.

2 Heat the vegetable oil in a frying pan (skillet), add the pork and fry over a medium–high heat for 10–12 minutes before adding the onion, black pudding, the chilli, ginger and garlic pastes, cumin seeds and chilli powder. Fry over a medium–high heat, stirring, making sure the pork and black pudding crisp and colour, and the spices do not burn. Add the garam masala to finish, along with a generous pinch of salt.

3 To serve, spread the hummus over a plate or bowl, creating a little well inside. Turn the sizzling keema into the middle of the dish, sprinkle with toasted sesame seeds and a little more chopped coriander. Top with amchoor onions.

Quick
& Light

"

Dishes designed to involve a little less chopping, stirring or tending to – without compromising on flavour or joy. You can get ahead on next-day prep or assemble at the last moment and some you can eat out of the pan.

I would like to tell you that I have all the time in a day to cook and labour over my meals in the kitchen but I have to be a little realistic. I learnt early on from my mother that a few little cheats to get ahead could mean you can assemble dinner pretty quickly. This is when building up your kitchen pyar really repays you, helping out when you're time-pushed. This isn't fast food but it's certainly a little quicker!

These dishes have the same flavour and vibrancy of the other dishes in this book but hopefully they come with a more manageable time covenant to land them. They can double up as working lunches to see you through the week – and, mixed with 'bits on the side', they can keep you going with plenty of variation.

Even when I'm cooking for just me I like to make something that's really delicious. Often the perception is that South Asian food takes an age to prep and cook and so maybe you only cook it for a large gathering. This couldn't be further from the truth so this is a great opportunity to use your spices midweek with healthy, fresh light cooking and hopefully give yourself a lunch upgrade too.

There is enough flexibility in the delivery of these dishes that you can serve them in a more relaxed fashion – or you can take time to plate them. Also, this is the time to break a few rules and mix and match proteins and pulses –whatever works for you!

roasted bream, fennel & tamarind tomato

This is about as quick as fish supper can be really. I have always loved bream and once upon a time it was less expensive than sea bass but with the same sort of flavour. You can use whatever fish you like but I really love the crispy skin and translucent flesh with the fresh tanginess of fennel and tamarind. Should you want to turn this into a large feast, you can scale up the marinade and put it on half a side of salmon before baking.

SERVES | 4 GENEROUSLY

4 fillets bream or red snapper (or other portioned firm fish), skin on

½ tsp ground cumin

½ tsp amchoor (dried mango powder)

6 tbsp vegetable oil

2 fennel bulb

Zest and juice of 1 unwaxed lemon

300g (11oz) ripe cherry tomatoes

6 finely chopped spring onions (scallions)

6 tbsp freshly chopped coriander (cilantro)

1 tsp finely chopped green chilli

6 tbsp tamarind sauce

½ tsp ground turmeric

½ tsp garam masala

8 tbsp olive oil

Sea salt (kosher salt)

1 Check the fish has no bones or scales. Put the cumin, amchoor and ¼ teaspoon of salt in a shallow dish with 1 tablespoon of the vegetable oil. Lay the fish flesh-side down in the marinade and coat well. Set aside or, if you're doing this a day ahead, cover and pop it in the fridge.

2 Finely slice the fennel on a mandolin or on the slicing side of your grater. Pop into a bowl and add the lemon zest and juice along with ½ teaspoon of salt. This can sit for about 15–20 minutes, allowing the fennel to soften in the marinade.

3 Chop your cherry tomatoes into small dice or quarter each one. Put into a bowl with the chopped spring onion, coriander, chilli and tamarind sauce. Mix well and set aside (you don't want this to be fridge cold).

4 Heat the remaining vegetable oil over a medium heat in a non-stick frying pan (skillet). Gently lay down the fish, skin-side down, placing it away from you so the hot oil does not splash. Cook over a low–medium heat until the skin is crispy and the flesh begins to turn translucent almost all the way through.

5 Turn the fillet over for a final minute before removing from the heat.

6 Put the fennel on plates, top with the fish and a few generous spoonfuls of your tomato dressing.

smoked haddock kedgeree

This is so easy to make, really delicious and super comforting. I like to use lightly smoked haddock or cod, but if you fancy using trout, or even fresh salmon or cod, that's fine – just season it with salt. I use a pouch of microwave brown rice because that way I can get it to the table in record time but you can use leftover cooked rice or even cooked orzo if you fancy. This dish was one my mother adored – and most people have a version they gravitate towards. For me, it has to be smoked fish and always a soft egg.

SERVES | 4 (OR 2 GREEDILY WITH LEFTOVERS FOR LUNCH)

50ml (¼ cup) vegetable oil

1 medium white onion, finely sliced

5 curry leaves

1 cassia bark stick

4 green cardamom pods

500g (1lb 2oz) lightly smoked haddock or cod

50g (1¾oz) butter

1 heaped tsp garam masala

1 tsp amchoor (dried mango powder)

1 tsp ground coriander

1 tsp ground cumin

1 tsp finely chopped Indian green chilli

2 tbsp ginger paste

500g (1lb 2oz) microwave rice (you can use brown or basmati)

3 spring onions (scallions), washed and finely sliced

Generous sprinkle of roughly chopped coriander (cilantro)

2 tbsp crispy onions/shallots

1 large lemon

Salt

4 free-range eggs, soft-boiled or poached, to serve

1 Heat the oil in a large shallow frying pan (skillet). Add the onion, curry leaves, cassia bark and green cardamom pods and fry over a medium heat until the onion begins to colour.

2 Meanwhile, cook the smoked haddock or cod with the slice of butter under a preheated grill (broiler) on high for 10 minutes to cook the fish through. When done, remove and carefully break into large flakes.

3 Add the ground spices, chilli and ginger paste to the pan and fry for a further 5 minutes.

4 Heat the microwave rice and stir well into the pan before adding the flaked fish. Once you have added the fish, stir carefully so you don't break all the flakes.

5 Finish with a pinch of salt, the chopped spring onions, fresh coriander, crispy shallots and a big squeeze of lemon juice.

6 I like to soft-boil the eggs but you can poach them if you prefer. This dish calls for being dressed in the pan and sent straight to the table for maximum joy and minimal faff. Soft eggs or poached eggs give a great self sauce but, if you like, add a dollop of tempered spice yoghurt.

lindi pepper poussin

I really love Lindi pepper. It has an amazing floral spice and when you pair this with a malai-style yoghurt-marinated poussin it makes a knockout dish. Barbecued little spicy chickens can only be a good idea. If you want to roast them in the oven, though, you absolutely can. Marinating them for two days helps to really impart the flavour but if you want to do this a few hours before, of course you can. Equally you can use boneless chicken breasts for a much faster supper.

SERVES | 2

2 poussin

MARINADE

4 tbsp full-fat Greek-style yoghurt

2 tsp ground lindi pepper

Juice of ½ lime

½ tsp ground cumin

½ tsp garam masala

1 tsp garlic paste

2 tsp ginger paste

1 tsp Indian green chilli paste

1 tsp salt

1 tbsp rapeseed (canola) oil

1 Combine all the marinade ingredients in a mixing bowl large enough to fit in both your poussin.

2 Score into the thigh and breast of the poussin to a depth of about 1cm (½in).

3 Pop into the marinade and really rub the yoghurt and spices into the birds.

4 Cover tightly and leave to marinate in the fridge for up to 48 hours.

5 Cook on a hot barbecue for 30 minutes, turning regularly to make sure the poussin cook evenly. If you are roasting in the oven, cook at 180°C fan/200°C/400°F/gas mark 6 for 1 hour. To check the birds are cooked, pierce the thickest part of the thigh: the juices should run clear. Allow to rest for 15 minutes.

6 Serve either with fresh green chutney (see page 172), naans and salads or shred the meat from the bone and load into delicious rolls or baguettes and top with chutney or achaari mayo (see page 176).

prawn, spring onion & curry leaf pancakes

There is something very special about a prawn pancake – and this one is both familiar and a hybrid at the same time. Effectively a thin spiced egg batter holds it all together, and a lot of spring onions and prawns. I like to eat mine drizzled with some crispy garlic chilli oil (see page 177).

SERVES | 2

50g (1¾oz) gram flour, sifted

4 tbsp water

2 free-range eggs

1 tsp salt

1 tsp ginger paste

2 green chillies, finely sliced

½ tsp ground coriander

½ tsp garam masala

½ tsp black pepper

10 fresh curry leaves, finely shredded

1 bunch of spring onions (scallions), trimmed

500g (1lb 2oz) peeled raw prawns (shrimp)

Small handful of chopped coriander (cilantro)

Vegetable oil, for frying

1 In a bowl, mix together the gram flour, water and eggs until smooth. Add the salt, ginger paste, chillies, spices and curry leaves.

2 Cut each spring onion into thirds, retaining the green tops, then in half lengthways. Wash well and drain on paper towels.

3 Split the prawns (shrimp) lengthways as if you were butterflying them but cut them into two.

4 Add the spring onions, prawns and coriander to the batter and mix well.

5 Heat 1 teaspoon of oil in a non-stick frying pan (skillet) over a medium–high heat. Add a couple of large spoonfuls of the batter, tilting the pan to form a pancake (crêpe). Turn after a minute or two and cook the other side for a further couple of minutes. Repeat until all the batter is used, oiling the pan each time.

6 Remove from the heat and eat with chutneys, achaari mayo or with the crispy garlic chilli oil (see pages 172–177).

The Stag Hunt Inn
Usha James

I visited Usha at her pub The Stag Hunt Inn in Ponsanooth, Cornwall. As some of you know, I really do have a soft spot for a great pub, especially if there may be something a little different to be found coming out of the kitchen. Usha's pub is exactly this: delicious home-cooked South Asian food, warm and very welcoming. When she moved from the Midlands to Cornwall with her husband Garry 25 years ago, her intention was to start her own business. After 9 years in Cornwall, when the village pub came up for sale, Usha planned to buy the pub, find a chef and perhaps take more of a landlady approach to the business. As it transpired, this was not to be and for many reasons she found herself in the kitchen at the helm of her new ship.

Usha had in mind a menu of really good rustic pub food – it was, after all, the era of the gastro pub – and she was not initially keen to do a curry night, despite the demand. The problem she saw was that most people's idea of curry was what they ate in the curry houses of the time, or those made with ready-made pastes. These didn't capture the beauty or essence of the curries Indian people have grown up with, nor did she know how to cook them. Cornwall didn't have a wide range of ethnic restaurants, so her cooking would be something new – and a bit of a gamble. She made a deal with the customers: she would do curry nights, but it would be the curries she grew up with alongside dishes she created herself at home, not typical restaurant curries like chicken tikka masala. As it turned out, this became an opportunity for people to enter the world of spice and for Usha to share her Gujarati cuisine. As her reputation grew, one curry night was not enough. The curry menu now runs all week alongside a traditional pub menu, plus specials cooked by her son Daniel, so there is something for everyone, young and old.

We cooked a beautiful fish curry together, full of unbelievably fresh local Cornish fish and enjoyed our lunch with hot buttery parathas and abundant chat. She speaks of how locally she doesn't have the same infrastructure that she had in the Midlands for all of her spices and ingredients, but how online shopping has been able to gap-fill for what she is missing. It does remind me how lucky I am for all that is so easily available to me in Wolverhampton and Tooting High Street – and that while fundamentally it provides excellent ingredients essential for South Asian cookery, it also provides a solid and established community that has been built to sustain our culture. I make a note to bring a care package of wholesale spices, curry leaves and dry store essentials on my next trip to Cornwall! It strikes me how brave and pioneering Usha has been, to carve herself a space locally to cook the food she loves that means something to her. Food has enabled her to find a point of difference for her business, to celebrate her culture and also to show people what real home cooking is.

As we chat about tradition, authenticity and what it means to create in the kitchen, she is wonderfully pragmatic about food. She cooks for people to enjoy, without ego, but with a kind of considered acknowledgement of all of the delicious things she grew up eating – and a respect for her ingredients. She cooks freely,

> **"**
> Every time I cook, I think about my mother.

> **"**
> Every time I reach into my spice tin, I think of everyone I have learnt from.

> "It's not always about using the most expensive ingredients. You can make an incredible Indian dish with cheap ingredients if you know what to do with your spices.

without rules and regulations and prioritizes enjoyment! As the pub became established as one that served Desi food, people wanted to see more choices and got a little braver with their requests for new dishes, of which Usha happily provided.

A signature dish of dai ki murgi came about when she wanted to introduce people to the flavour of a traditional Gujarati chicken curry. At home she eats it with a side of yoghurt, and so she decided to cook it with a touch of yoghurt and cream to give the sauce more body. Unsurprisingly it was a hit with her customers. She sometimes compares her curries to Thai curries, with similar freshness and that punch of 'garlic, ginger and chillies that dance on the tongue'. I particularly love her use of local meats, seafood and, of course, some seriously remarkable Cornish dairy products!

It was Usha's mother who taught her how to cook, and her mother was taught by her grandmother, and on goes the handing-down of knowledge and recipes between generations. We talked a lot about this and what it means to us to cook recipes that were passed down to us at difficult times of our lives. There is power in being able to cook dishes that bring people nearer to you, even back to you. There is an opportunity, we agreed, for us both to reframe sadness and loss by recreating dishes that are just so delicious and abundantly full of love that you have to smile. Through this nattering it was impossible not to laugh at the way in which we were both taught how to cook, and how information is passed down. No emails, no little books full of recipes and ingredients, no cookery videos – we learnt by being shown. This brings us to what Usha calls the 'Spice Dance'. This has nothing to do with a pop group but everything to do with the complexities of having to absorb ingredients and techniques to cook like your mother, at the stove, in real time. As Usha watched her mother cook, in went a spoon of this, two

spoons of that, a pinch of this, and as each item was added to the pot, there would be a moment where she would bring the spoon back to the masala tin and shake a little off, or put a bit more in, making it nigh on impossible to work out an accurate measurement. We also haven't even touched on the marvellous array of non-spoon 'spoons' used to make the task even harder: Calpol spoons, coffee scoops, spoon handles – you name it. And really I think this is the bit that perhaps means that we are all always a fraction off an exact replica of the original classic anyway – so now you have to work extra hard to remember how it tasted, not just how it was cooked!

Usha cooks, as she says, 'from a Gujarati spice foundation, looking through Indian eyes at recipes from all over the world'. She particularly loves riffing seaside classics into remarkable spiced versions – something else that gives her such a mark of difference. Dishes such as: roasted mackerel, Bombay potatoes, horseradish raita and beetroot relish; oven-roasted cod or sea bass and prawns (shrimp) on dhal, which is cooked with shell-on prawns for flavour; pan-fried langoustines with turmeric, garlic, ginger and chilli with a crusty bread; Bombay potato, crab and fresh mango; breast of lamb stuffed with sag aloo, harissa yoghurt and garlic and thyme paratha; aubergine salaan and cannellini beans in a coconut, peanut and sesame sauce; Haggis keema, Christmas pudding kulfi... her creativity is endless. It seems clear to me that Usha too loves to dance in the magical area between traditional past and playful future. She spoke warmly, authentically and excitedly about food and the parts of her culture that she loves the most – and it is impossible not to share with her the feeling of 'privilege at our culinary heritage'. No matter what the next chapter has in store for Usha and her cooking, it is sure to be delicious.

spiced squash & broccoli salad, dukkah & coconut yoghurt

This is a really easy salad, great for a quick dinner or to have as a barbecue side. Just double up if you're having friends over – and plate on a big platter for the wow factor. This is one of those dishes that can become a centrepiece with additional 'bits on the side' or work nicely as a side itself. I encourage plating up to share!

SERVES | 2 AS A MAIN OR 4 AS A SIDE

1 small butternut squash peeled, halved, seeds removed and cut into 2cm (1in) slices

2 large red onions, peeled and cut into 6 wedges

4 tbsp vegetable oil

Sea salt (kosher salt)

½ tsp amchoor (dried mango powder)

1 tsp cumin seeds

½ tsp ground coriander

½ tsp chilli flakes

200g (7oz) tenderstem broccoli

100g (scant ½ cup) coconut yoghurt

Fresh coriander (cilantro), to garnish

DUKKAH

2 tbsp olive oil

1 tsp garlic paste

1 tsp chilli paste

6 fresh curry leaves

½ tsp black mustard seeds

1 Preheat the oven to 180°C fan/200°C/400°F/gas mark 6. Put the squash and onions in a big bowl along with the oil, salt and spices. Mix well and turn into a baking tray. Cook for about 20 minutes until the squash is tender and the onions are roasted nicely.

2 Meanwhile, blanch the broccoli in boiling salted water for 2 minutes and drain: you don't want it to be too soft, otherwise you lose all the texture. Set aside.

3 To make the dukkah, put the olive oil in a small pan or frying pan (skillet) with the garlic and chilli pastes, the curry leaves and mustard seeds. Cook over a medium heat until the mustard seeds start to pop, the curry leaves sizzle and you can smell the garlic. Remove from the heat and stir gently into your yoghurt.

4 To assemble the salad, plate up the roasted vegetables and broccoli, drizzle with the yoghurt and garnish with chopped coriander.

aloo gobi hash, fried egg & green chutney

Aloo gobi deserves a medal for its unwavering glory. It has been a staple sabji for so many of us, long before the bandwagon for cauliflower 'steaks' and cauliflower everything took off. I have never met a gobi I didn't love. Tray-roasting the cauliflower makes it super easy and gives an amazing flavour and texture.

SERVES | 2

HASH

2 medium potatoes, cut into 4–6 pieces

1 small cauliflower, trimmed

1 medium white onion, sliced

Vegetable oil

¼ tsp ground turmeric

½ tsp cumin seeds

¼ tsp ground coriander

¼ tsp chilli powder

½ tsp black mustard seeds

½ tsp fennel seeds

1 garlic clove, minced

Small knob of fresh ginger, julienned

1 fresh chilli, finely chopped

1 lemon, for squeezing

Salt

TO SERVE (OPTIONAL)

¼ bunch of fresh coriander (cilantro), to serve

2 free-range eggs, poached or fried

Fresh green chutney (see page 172)

1 Preheat the oven to 180°C fan/200°C/400°F/gas mark 6.

2 Par-boil the potatoes and drain (or use cooked leftovers if you have any). Break down the cauliflower, retaining the tender inner leaves. Roughly chop these and pop onto a large baking tray. Break the cauliflower head into florets, roughly chop the stalk into small dice and add to the baking tray, along with the sliced onion. Generously drizzle with vegetable oil and sprinkle with your spices. Add the garlic, ginger and chilli. Mix well in the baking tray.

3 Roast for about 30 minutes – you want the cauliflower to colour and burnish slightly, which will add flavour. Squeeze over the lemon.

4 I like to serve my hash with some fresh coriander and a fried egg for an easy lunch or supper – should you have some, a little green chutney tastes amazing too!

punjabi panzanella, kalonji & crispy channa

I feel almost religious in my adoration for panzanella. I absolutely adore the food of Tuscany and I really feel this tremendously frugal dish made with stale bread connects hugely with the agriculture of Punjab. Respect for homegrown ingredients, seasonality and no waste is something most cooks from rural areas have been championing for generations. There are but a few ingredients here, with only one very important deal-breaker: this must not be refrigerated – chilling steals flavour, texture and the personality from a ripe tomato.

SERVES | 2

Handful of stale bread (naan, ciabatta, sourdough or, if you only have sliced, that's OK too)

Olive oil

1 garlic clove

1 medium red onion, finely sliced

Sea salt (kosher salt)

2 tbsp sherry vinegar

300g (10½oz) tomatoes – the ripest you can find

1 tsp chaat masala

½ tsp nigella seeds (kalonji)

A little fresh coriander (cilantro)

CRISPY CHANNA

½ can chickpeas (garbanzo beans), drained

½ tsp salt

½ tsp chilli powder

1 tsp garam masala

1 Preheat the oven to 180°C fan/200°C/400°F/gas mark 6 and line a baking tray with baking paper. Put the chickpeas in a bowl with the salt, chilli powder and garam masala and turn to combine. Spread out on the lined tray and roast for 30–40 minutes until crunchy and golden. Tip into a bowl and set aside.

2 Meanwhile, tear up your bread, spread over the same baking tray and drizzle with some olive oil. Bash the garlic clove and give it a good mix around with the bread. Toast in the oven for about 8 minutes until it is crispy but not totally brittle.

3 In a large bowl, mix the onion, sea salt and sherry vinegar well.

4 Now, roughly chop your tomatoes. It's really important to transfer all of the tomato juice from the chopping board to the bowl, along with the tomatoes, as this becomes your dressing.

5 Add the toasted bread to the bowl with the chaat masala and nigella seeds. Mix really well before adding the crispy chickpeas and chopped coriander. Add a glug more olive oil and sherry vinegar and mix well. Leave for at least 15 minutes (if you can) before enjoying.

achari baked fish

This dish is really quick to prepare. It almost self sauces with the pickle and the juice from the fish and you can have it with any number of 'bits on the side'.

SERVES | 2

4 spring onions (scallions)

2 fillets or portions of firm fish (try salmon, cod or hake), preferably skinned

3 tbsp your favourite achaar or pickle

1 tsp olive oil

Tempered spice slaw (see page 192)

1 Preheat the oven to 180°C fan/200°C/400°F/gas mark 6.

2 Slice the spring onions lengthways and wash thoroughly. Add to an ovenproof dish.

3 Sit the fish in the dish, spread the achaar over it and drizzle the spring onions and fish with olive oil.

4 Bake for about 12–15 minutes until the fish is cooked through.

5 I like to serve this with the tempered spice slaw.

roasted vegetable chaat

Chaat for me is the opportunity to give any fruit or vegetable dish a superpower with extra texture, flavour and immediate good vibes. This again stems from the initial investment in your cupboard spices which allows you to make something fairly mundane really special. I have deliberately used readily available root veg – but use what you like. My preference for a roasted chaat is to use veg that sweeten when roasted, and also hold their form.

SERVES | 4

2 red-skinned potatoes, peeled

2 carrots, peeled

2 red onions, quartered

1 small cauliflower, trimmed and broken into florets

1 sweetheart (hispi) cabbage

SPICING

2 tsp ginger paste

2 tsp green chilli paste

1 tsp garlic paste

4 tbsp vegetable oil

1½ tsp ground cumin

1 tsp Kashmiri chilli powder

1½ tsp garam masala

FROM YOUR CUPBOARD

Chaat masala

Tamarind sauce

Crispy sev/papdi

TO SERVE

Natural (plain) or Greek-style yoghurt

Spring onion (scallion), finely chopped

Fresh coriander (cilantro)

Fresh green chilli, finely chopped, optional

1 Preheat the oven to 180°C fan/200°C/400°F/gas mark 6. Cut the potatoes into 3cm (1¼in) cubes, cover with cold salted water and bring to the boil. Cook for 8 minutes or so before draining well.

2 This is the fun part. Line the biggest baking tray that fits in your oven with baking paper. Cut the carrots lengthways, then into 4cm (1½in) batons. Spread them out, along with the onions, cauliflower, cabbage and potatoes, over the baking tray.

3 Mix all the spicing ingredients together and drizzle over the veg, mixing well.

4 Roast for about 20–25 minutes – you want some colouration and burnishing of the vegetables, which gives all the flavour.

5 When everything is tender but retains its structure, remove the tray from the oven.

6 Season again with chaat masala. To serve, drizzle liberally with tamarind sauce and yoghurt and scatter on some crispy sev, spring onion and fresh coriander. If you like it a little spicier, add some finely chopped green chilli.

Short Eats
Melissa Bakth

Melissa and I meet at her home in the Barbican in London, and as soon as I arrive, there is a wondrous welcome committee of her and her two gorgeous children. I get hugs, and already I feel like I am home. Melissa has a mixed Sri Lankan and Trinidadian heritage and she is all about food. She too enjoys the technicolour landscape of being a 'third-culture kid', dipping and dabbling into all the culinary influences available to her. She says she is all about 'old-school cooking with a new school of thought', and this is why I am here. 'I learnt everything I know about Sri Lankan cooking from sitting in the kitchen with my grandparents and dad while they cooked. The aromas that filled the kitchen smelled intoxicating and the taste was magical. When I started cooking I began to tweak classic recipes to add my own stamp on things.' Back in the 70s, a mutual friend introduced her mum to 'this guy who makes really good curries'; in a nutshell, this was where it all started. When her parents got together, there was a marriage of love, culture and flavour. Melissa tells me it has always been all about food in her family.

Growing up, she recalls how her father had specific Sri Lankan dishes he would cook, and her mother cooked specific dishes from Trinidad. Melissa would watch all of this happen in front of her and was spellbound. Same ingredients, twice cooked with fantastical differences. Her number one favourites were 'short eats', a little assortment of delicious small plates designed to whet the appetite. To her, life was 'just a series of Short Eats' – and so the name of her company was born. Melissa would come home from school,

hearing about beans on toast and fish fingers, and her parents would riff off the classics but adding spices and chillies so this became her version of classics, now the norm in her own repertoire. Along with her parents, Melissa's aunt was a huge influence, adding a Sri Lankan–Malaysian inspiration to her cooking. When she married her Bangladeshi husband, there was yet another amazing cuisine to explore and adopt.

As a mum to two young children, Melissa has a zen-like calm when in the kitchen. She talks me through her love of great, fresh home-cooked food, and that the kids are allowed to not like things, but they must try them. And while we cook together, there is avid interest from both her daughter and her son about what's happening, and what might be ready for tasting. There is something special about being involved when you're young – in the kitchen, in laying the table and, of course, getting involved at the table. Hospitality was a craft learnt at home and mastered in restaurants for me. And it was being in the kitchen at home with my mother that ignited my passion for cooking – and also my appetite when it came to eating.

Melissa began in a graphic design agency before making a break into food. She started to write about food, cook more and have a creative outlet for her love of food. Her client list naturally took a turn to working with various food and drink brands until she finally transitioned to her own business. Melissa thought it was time to make the jump – and she started Short Eats, a pop-up that was big on music, big on flavour and created a feasting

> **"**
> I learnt everything I
> know about Sri Lankan
> cooking from sitting
> in the kitchen with my
> grandparents and dad
> while they cooked.

carnival vibe. She loves to feed and also loves the idea of people having a seriously jolly time. When lockdown struck she moved to meal kits and ready meals delivered locally, to maintain her cooking fix and to look after people in her community. Many people asked for South Asian mini-meals for children, and this is now something she is championing – kids food with a Sri Lankan twist. How lucky her little ones are to be guinea pigs on the testing of all this deliciousness! 'The most popular dishes in our kids' range is our mango and coconut hoppers and red rice and banana rotis – both light and fluffy' – something totally different for kids to try. She says that 'we should start kids off in the right way' by which she means aware, excited and enjoying all foods, including food from their culture. Her goal is to bring accessibility and convenience to this market, and not have to sacrifice flavour for convenience. The whole point is to be offering interesting, exciting food groups for babies and young children, that help them establish tools to make 'healthy balanced and adventurous decisions as adults', and simultaneously keep them connected to their cultures. I think a lot about meals my niece eats, and how great it would be if there were some more interesting South Asian dishes to get excited about rather than just the usual run of 'kids' food', which is often uninspiring.

On the stove there is a creamy dhal, aubergine curry (a signature dish), spicy chickpeas, greens and spiced squash, all to be served around rice with beetroot pickle. In her store cupboard Melissa introduces me to a salted, air-dried green chilli I have never seen before. It is smoky, sweet, salty and has an incredible heat. This is one of those moments where I am sure I may never have come across these chillies unless they were introduced to me by someone. We toast them off and crush them to season the dish at the end, along with some beautifully sweet coconut. Collaborations and conversations create opportunities for discovery, and here I am yet again seeing something totally new to me!

When we start to talk about cooking and indeed eating habits, Melissa tells me she finds 'the culture of going to a restaurant and ordering one curry with rice, really strange. That's just not how we eat! You should have a little bit of everything and you get to enjoy all of it.' I couldn't agree more, and this leads to a hugely animated conversation about the importance of who your dinner companions might be. If you're not sharing, you're not caring, and we can't be friends. Simple.

As she talks me through the plating, she talks about a colour wheel, no doubt helping her little ones engage in their food, but also reflecting the vibrancy and variation of good

things to come. Rice is plated in the middle of the dish, with six different items spooned around the outside and there is much to be excited about! I start to try things individually, but Melissa encourages me to get stuck in, taking a little of everything, mixing it into the rice and eating it together. The whole point she tells me, is that 'everything goes so well together', and it really does. This is a really comforting plate of food, completely vegan, completely delicious. As we enjoy lunch, her children come to try everything, cautiously picking out any chilli and getting stuck in, it's just wonderful to see. Short Eats, Long Eats, if Melissa is cooking, I am in.

THE only dhal you'll ever need

I have lost track of how many people have asked me for a dhal recipe. As a child, I completely undervalued dhal, not because it wasn't utterly delicious but because it seemed so regular, accessible and so normal. As an adult it has been an absolute joy to learn how to cook it properly and to keep refining my recipe. Tarka dhal brings me a particular kind of comfort, unmatched by any other dish. For those who haven't much experience, masoor or toor dhal is one I would recommend you practise with first, predominantly as it is inexpensive and doesn't require soaking or slow cooking. Batch-cook it once a month and you'll never be stuck for an obscenely delicious dinner again. If you have any curry leaves, you could pop these into the tarka but I promise the dish won't be any less amazing if you don't. Vegan friends: please make the tarka without butter – you can replace it with a teaspoon of coconut or vegetable oil.

SERVES | 4

200g (7oz) masoor dhal (red split lentils)

4 tbsp vegetable oil

1 large white onion, finely sliced or chopped

2 tsp green chilli paste

2 tsp ginger paste

1 tsp garlic paste

½ tsp ground turmeric

1 tsp ground cumin

1 tsp ground coriander

1 tsp garam masala

Fresh coriander (cilantro)

Salt

TARKA, TO FINISH

20g (¾oz) butter

1 green chilli, sliced at an angle

1 garlic clove, finely sliced

1 small thumb of fresh ginger, julienned or finely chopped

1 heaped tsp cumin seeds

Curry leaves, optional

1 Put your lentils in a sieve (strainer) and rinse under the cold tap until the water is clear and not cloudy. Pop into a saucepan with 400ml (1¾ cups) cold water and bring to the boil with a wooden spoon resting across the pan (this should stop the overboil). The lentils should take about 15–20 minutes to cook through, until they break easily between your fingers and don't leave a chalky residue.

2 Meanwhile, put the oil in another pan and add the onion and begin to cook out – this will take about 15 minutes if you have sliced it finely. Add the chilli, ginger and garlic pastes and cook out for a further 8 minutes or so. Add ½ teaspoon salt and turn off the heat.

3 Add the onion mix to the pan of lentils and stir well.

4 For the tarka, melt the butter in the pan used to cook the onions, add the rest of the tarka ingredients and heat over a medium–high heat until they begin to sizzle. The butter should brown but not burn and you must catch the garlic before it burns but after it colours. When the butter is foaming, turn the tarka into the dhal, mixing well.

5 Add the garam masala, salt to taste and some fresh coriander.

coconut pork tenderloin, spinach & sweet potato

This is a really nice speedy dish for midweek. If you don't fancy tenderloin, you can use a chop, or belly slices, which will need to cook for a little longer. What I love most is the little cheat to a super-flavoursome curry sauce, without the labour of slow-cooking onions to build depth of flavour. Again, there really is no reason why this wouldn't work for tofu, paneer, cauliflower or indeed chicken or fish.

SERVES | 2

1 pork tenderloin, approx. 500g (1lb 2oz)

2 medium sweet potatoes

2 tbsp vegetable oil

Pinch of sea salt (kosher salt)

½ tsp ground cumin

Baby spinach

MARINADE

1 can coconut cream

3 tbsp ginger paste

2 tbsp green chilli paste

2 tsp garlic paste

4 curry leaves

1 level tsp ground turmeric

1 tsp ground cumin

2 tsp ground coriander

1 tsp Kashmiri chilli powder

6 spring onions (scallions), washed, peeled and chopped

1 tsp black mustard seeds

1 tsp garam masala

1 tsp salt

Juice of 1 lemon

1 Make the marinade by combining all the ingredients. You can pour this into a ziplock bag and put the pork into it a day ahead but if you're pushed for time, you can just put everything into a baking tray, providing your pork will fit in it, along with the marinade.

2 When you are ready to cook, preheat the oven to 180°C fan/ 200°C/400°F/gas mark 6. Peel your sweet potatoes before cutting into wedges (not too chunky otherwise they won't cook at the same time as the pork). Dress them with the oil, salt and ground cumin and spread out over another baking tray.

3 Pop both trays into the oven and cook for about 30–35 minutes or until the pork is cooked through and your wedges are tender.

4 Ten minutes before the end of the cook time, stir the spinach through the sauce.

5 Serve the pork tenderloin, sliced, with the sweet potato wedges and a generous spoon of the curry sauce.

cumin-spiced lamb skewers with smashed aubergine

This is super quick because the meat is easy to prep and, as with the other kebabs in this book, you can always make patties or burgers if you don't fancy the faff of skewers (although my tip is to invest in some steel skewers as they reduce the cook time drastically by cooking the meat from the inside out). So, enter a holy trinity of flavours: lamb, aubergine (eggplant) and spices – a triumph.

SERVES | 2

500g (1lb 2oz) minced (ground) lamb

1 medium white onion, finely diced

2 tbsp ginger paste

1 heaped tsp finely chopped Indian chilli

1½ tsp garam masala

2 tsp amchoor (dried mango powder)

1 tsp ground coriander

1 tsp ground cumin

1½ tsp salt

2 small pinches of fresh coriander (cilantro), chopped

50ml (¼ cup) vegetable oil

SMASHED AUBERGINE

2 large aubergines (eggplant)

Olive oil

1 white onion, finely sliced

1 tsp ginger

½ tsp cumin seeds

Juice of 1 lemon

Handful of pomegranate seeds

1 tsp garlic

1 Put the lamb, onion, ginger and garlic into a large bowl. Add all the dried spices, salt and fresh coriander.

2 Oil your hands using a little of the vegetable oil, then divide the mix into four and shape around your metal skewers. You can use soaked wooden bamboo skewers too, but equally to avoid burning them and the faff, roll the mix into 6 balls and gently flatten into patties. These will work well on the barbecue or under the grill (broiler).

3 Roast your aubergines in a dry pan or over a gas flame until charred heavily. They should almost collapse on themselves when they are done; if you need to show them to the oven, 10 minutes at 180°C fan/200°C/400°F/gas mark 6 can help them along. Split them open and scoop out the flesh into a bowl.

4 Put the oil in a large frying pan (skillet) and add the onion, ginger and cumin seeds. Fry on a medium–high heat so that the onion colours well. At this point add the aubergine flesh and sauté, mixing well. Season. After about 4–5 minutes, remove from the heat, add the lemon juice, chopped coriander and pomegranate seeds.

5 Cook your kebabs on a preheated barbecue for 10–15 minutes. Kebabs on metal skewers take less time than wooden ones, so keep checking and cook a for little longer if you need.

6 Serve on top of a few spoons of smashed aubergine with fresh green chutney (see page 172), naans and salad.

lamb chops with green chutney potato salad

Lamb is a special occasion meat for me. I'm not sure why but it feels very celebratory, and chops are delicious. You get to enjoy the tender eye of the fillet, but the best bit for me is the meat that runs along the rib, that you can only really enjoy if you commit to picking them up with your hands and getting stuck in. The marinade here can work for paneer, fish, chicken or even over a cauliflower. Whatever you do – make these potatoes, and don't be tempted to put them in the fridge – ambient is best for all of the magic. This is my mum's recipe – and I haven't met anyone who doesn't love it.

SERVES | 2

6 lamb chops

200g (7oz) new potatoes
(young waxy potatoes)

6 tbsp fresh green chutney
(see page 172)

MARINADE

2 tsp ginger paste

½ tsp green chilli paste

½ tsp freshly ground black pepper

½ tsp salt

2 tbsp vegetable oil

½ tsp ground turmeric

½ tsp garam masala

½ tsp cumin seeds

3 tbsp natural (plain) yoghurt

1 To make the marinade, put all the ingredients in a bowl. Mix well and add the chops. You can do this a couple of days ahead of schedule for the best results.

2 Cut your potatoes into even pieces (in half is fine) and put into a pan of cold salted water. Bring to the boil and cook for 12–15 minutes.

3 When the potatoes are cooked through, drain and allow to steam in a colander. Shake well to encourage fluffiness before transferring to a bowl. Add the green chutney and mix well. Leave to one side until you're ready to serve.

4 Preheat the grill or a griddle pan (grill pan) until very hot. Cook your chops for 3–4 minutes per side, depending on their thickness and how well done you like them. When caramelized and burnished well, remove from the heat and allow to rest for about 5 minutes. During resting delicious juices are produced, which I recommend you pour over the chops when you plate. Serve with the potato salad.

Meals & Feasts

> "Dishes to share around a table full of friends.

There is something that is so intrinsic in me when it comes to feeding people. I can't help myself – I love it. It goes without saying that my childhood was full of various parties – weddings, family get-togethers and social events – which hinged heavily around food.

There was such generosity and abundance of food at these parties, and often this was very much the same when social events occurred at home. Giant pans of aloo gobi, rice, biriyani, dhal, sabji, yoghurt, rotis or naans – a riot of flavour that we were so very lucky was our norm. Buffet stations set up on trestle tables, dining tables and kitchen counters were eclipsed by huge pans covered in foil with enough food to feed a small country. I can't describe the excitement and anticipation of knowing there were so many delicious things to eat.

For me, feasting means sharing – often just going from pan to table and allowing everyone to get stuck in. I don't believe it means wedding-sized food portions, simply a pan of something put down for all to share. Arguably all these dishes can feature in a feasting fashion – and I encourage this wholeheartedly. This notion mostly comes from wanting to bring people together and, for me, to keep everyone around the table for as long as possible. Growing up, food wasn't really plated and portioned. It arrived on the middle of the table and helping yourself was the norm, plates being passed over each other, with various people taking charge to make sure that everyone had tried a bit of this sabji, that dhal, not forgetting the raita before eventually everyone would settle down to eat. Before long it would be time to ask if anyone wanted to have some more – 'gosh why aren't you eating enough?' – and then the goading from one roti, to have a half, at least a half, another spoon of dhal… it would be relentless until you caved in and surrendered to another helping.

There is a cultural nuance in South Asian homes. It spans generations – and I hope it will continue for many generations to come – and that is the desire to share. Share whatever you have – with those in need around you. No matter what was on the table it was shared with those who were visiting or just dropped in; it was done without a second's thought and with absolute sincerity. It is such a warm and welcoming manner, one I am tremendously proud of.

There is something about being around the dining table that I love. Not just the being at the table, but the laying, the scene-setting. It carries suspense and excitement at what will arrive, and it is such a wonderful opportunity to express gratitude.

masala bouillabaise

This dish requires a sizeable amount of prep, and a fairly good amount of time in the kitchen, but it is really very special. You can make elements of it ahead of schedule to marinate and prepare but if you are looking for something to make that really feels like a celebration, then give it a go. I like to make this with a glass of something crisp and cold in hand – and to take my time.

SERVES | 4

1 carrot, peeled and cut into 1cm (½in) dice

2 celery sticks, cut into 1cm (½in) dice

3 medium red-skinned potatoes, peeled and cut into 1cm (½in) dice

12 shell-on raw tiger prawns (jumbo shrimp), peeled and deveined, shells and heads reserved

1 small monkfish tail, boned and cut into 2.5cm (1in) cubes

2 fillets sea bream or bass, skin on, cut in half widthways

3 tbsp vegetable oil

Fresh coriander (cilantro), to garnish

MARINADE

½ tsp Kashmiri chilli powder

½ tsp ground coriander

½ tsp ground cumin

½ tsp amchoor (dried mango powder)

½ tsp salt

2 tbsp vegetable oil

½ tsp ground ginger

1 Par-boil all the diced vegetables in a pan together for 5–7 minutes. Drain and set aside.

2 Meanwhile, pop all the prawns and fish in a bowl with the marinade ingredients, mix well and allow to marinate.

3 To make the base (ingredients overleaf), in a large heavy-bottomed saucepan, heat the oil, onion, fennel, carrots, celery and curry leaves. Once they start to sizzle, add the prawn shells. Cook over a medium heat for 10–15 minutes until you can really smell the shellfish aroma and the veg are soft and sizzling.

4 Add the chilli, ginger and garlic pastes, fennel seeds and cardamom pod. Cook out before turning up the heat and adding the wine. This should sizzle off and reduce into the base.

5 Add the passata. Cook for about 8–9 minutes until it has thickened, making sure you break down the prawn shells into the sauce.

6 Add the turmeric, Kashmiri chilli and coconut cream, followed by the stock. Cook for about 10–15 minutes over a low–medium heat.

7 Pour through a strainer into another pan, using a ladle to push through all the liquid and break the prawn shells to release the flavour.

8 Add the garam masala, lime juice and your par-boiled veg, then leave to simmer, covered, over a low heat.

Continued overleaf

masala bouillabaise *continued*

BASE

6 tbsp vegetable oil

1 medium white onion, finely sliced

1 fennel bulb, finely sliced

2 carrots, finely sliced

2 large celery sticks, finely sliced

8 curry leaves

Shells reserved from the prawns (shrimp)

2 tsp green chilli paste

4 tsp ginger paste

3 tsp garlic paste

1 tsp fennel seeds

1 black cardamom pod

150ml (scant ⅔ cup) white wine (or champagne, but you can make it without)

110ml (scant ½ cup) passata (strained tomatoes)

½ tsp ground turmeric

1 tsp Kashmiri chilli powder

250ml (generous 1 cup) coconut cream

200ml (scant 1 cup) fish or chicken stock (bouillon)

2 tsp garam masala

Juice of 1½ limes

2 tsp salt

9 Meanwhile, add 3 tablespoons of oil to a large non-stick frying pan (skillet) and pan-fry your fish and shellfish for 4–5 minutes, making sure they develop a nice colour. I do this step because it makes it easier to assemble the dish and I love the crispy fish skin that develops, but you can always buy skinned fish and add it straight into the sauce.

10 Assemble by popping a few of the prawn and monkfish chunks in bowls, topping with a generous ladleful of the sauce and veg, and finishing with your crispy-skinned fish. Garnish with fresh coriander.

fish pulao

Fish with rice gives me the kind of comfort that dhal does. If you use microwave rice or leftover rice, you can get this done very quickly. Equally, if you commit to cooking your basmati, it's still on the table in about 30 minutes or so. Use whatever fish you can get hold of – add prawns if you like. It's key that you use raw fish so that by the time your rice finishes cooking, your fish is cooked too. I have used crispy onions in the base here because they save time and add a lovely sweetness to the rice, which works well with all the spiced elements. This is absolutely delicious with cauliflower, which you can cook through before adding to the rice.

SERVES | 2–4

FISH

400g (14oz) salmon, skinned, pin-boned and cut into 2.5cm (1in) cubes

2 tsp ground ginger

1 tsp green chilli paste

½ tsp ground turmeric

1 tsp amchoor (dried mango powder)

2 tbsp yoghurt

1 tbsp vegetable oil

Juice of ½ lime

½ tsp salt

1 tsp garam masala

1 tsp ground coriander

1 Marinate your fish in a bowl with all the ingredients. You can do this a day ahead if you need to (in which case, put the bowl in the fridge) but immediately before use will work too.

2 To start your pulao (see ingredients overleaf), put the oil in a frying pan (skillet) with a tight-fitting lid over a medium heat and add the cinnamon, cumin seeds, cardamom pods and allow to sizzle. Add the ginger and chilli pastes, and cook for 5 minutes, stirring well.

3 Add the crispy onions and salt, mix well before adding the rice, stir once and then add the water.

4 Increase the heat and bring to the boil – you want to stir only occasionally, until it looks like the water has almost all evaporated. You should be able to run your spoon through the rice and leave a channel.

Continued overleaf

fish pulao *continued*

PULAO

3 tbsp vegetable oil

1 cinnamon stick

2 tsp cumin seeds

4 green cardamom pods

2 tsp ginger paste

1 tsp green chilli paste

60g (2¼oz) crispy onions/shallots

1 tsp salt

250g (9oz) basmati rice (the best you can afford), rinsed well under cold water, then soaked for 15 minutes

300ml (1¼ cups) water

GARNISH

Fresh coriander (cilantro)

Sliced green chillies

Lime wedges

5 At this point, evenly scatter over your diced fish.

6 Turn the heat to the lowest setting, cover the rice with some baking paper or foil and then put the lid on tightly. Cook for 6 minutes on the lowest heat. Don't be tempted to open the lid or stir – you will lose heat and steam.

7 After 6 minutes, turn off the heat and leave it for 7–8 minutes.

8 Take the pan to the table, garnish with fresh coriander, chilli and lime wedges.

methi chicken Kyiv

Many of the dishes that we ate as children almost immediately became firm favourites and quite often they remain so as adults. There are two dishes that I particularly adored as a child: one was a garlic butter Kiev and the other was my mum's garlic methi chicken. I don't think we need to take too much time explaining why these two dishes can happily collaborate to create a garlic methi Kyiv. You can use fresh fenugreek but I particularly love the flavour of dried kasoori methi. If you want to have all of the flavour but don't have the patience for the process, then butterfly a chicken breast, flour, egg and breadcrumb it, and serve a slice of melting butter over it as a sort of Milanese schnitzel. Or, if you don't eat chicken, you can make the butter and melt it into jacket potatoes, over fish, paneer or other vegetables.

SERVES | 2

2 good-sized, skinless chicken breasts

6 tbsp plain (all-purpose) flour

2 eggs, beaten with a splash of milk

300g (10½oz) panko breadcrumbs

Salt and black pepper

Vegetable oil, for frying

BUTTER

150g (5½oz) salted butter, at room temperature

1 tsp kasoori methi (dried fenugreek)

1½ tsp garlic paste

2 tsp chopped coriander (cilantro) stalks

Pinch of black pepper

Zest of ½ unwaxed lemon

½ tsp green chilli paste

1 First, make the butter. Simply mash everything together and mix well. Lay a piece of cling film (plastic wrap) on your work surface. Spoon out the butter on to it to form a short line, then fold the cling film over it. Using the cling film to help you, roll the butter into a sausage shape about 1–1.5cm (½–⅝in) in width. This way there is no risk of having bits of cling film in your food.

2 Seal the ends of the sausage shape and put in the fridge for a few hours or overnight so the butter sets firm – this makes it far easier to stuff the chicken.

3 Insert the blade of a thin knife into the bigger end of each chicken breast to make a pocket in the middle: you don't want to pierce the skin otherwise your butter will ooze out. Remove the cling film from the butter and slice off about a 5cm (2in) piece. Insert into the pocket in the breast, then bring the meat together to ensure it remains closed. (You can also use 1 teaspoon of cornflour (corn starch) mixed with ½ teaspoon of water to create a little seal, if needed.)

4 Dip the chicken breasts first in seasoned flour, then in seasoned egg and finally coat in the breadcrumbs. Put them back in the fridge until you are ready to cook.

5 Preheat the oven to 180°C fan/200°C/400°F/gas mark 4. Pour enough vegetable oil to fill a deep frying pan (skillet) or saucepan by a third. Heat the oil and check the temperature by dropping in a little cube of bread: it should sizzle and turn a light golden colour. Very carefully lay in your chicken, one at a time if there is no space for both. Turn occasionally to ensure they fry and colour evenly. Remove and drain them on paper towels and then pop them into the oven for 15 minutes. Allow to rest for 5 minutes before serving.

masala pork belly

I absolutely adore pork belly – in all of its many variations. The layers of fat help keep the meat moist and it really stands up to big flavours. This technique was shown to me by my friend Karan Gokhani and I'm quite sure I won't make pork belly any other way now. It's so disheartening to have roast pork and not have crispy crackling – this way ensures you will always have success. Cook this as an alternative Sunday lunch serving with jeera roasties (see page 185), roasted chaat and chutneys or serve with mango salad, slaw and flatbreads for a delicious feast. The one important thing to note is that the pork benefits hugely from having time to dry out in your fridge for a day or two – this is one of the keys to a winning crunch.

SERVES | 4

800g (1lb 12oz) piece of pork belly (you can scale up the recipe)

1 tsp black cumin seeds

1 tsp coriander seeds

1 tsp amchoor (dried mango powder)

1 tsp salt

1 tsp chilli powder

½ tsp garam masala

1 tsp bicarbonate of soda (baking soda)

2 tsp white vinegar

1 You will need to pat dry your pork belly to make sure any excess liquid has been removed – paper towel is perfect for this.

2 Using a sharp knife, carefully score into the skin of your belly without cutting through too far into the fat and flesh. You can score however you please, but 1–1.5cm (½–⅝in) is a nice width between cuts. You can cross-hatch if you like, by scoring in the opposite direction – however you please.

3 Pop the belly on a tray or dish and leave, uncovered, in the bottom of the fridge for a day or two.

4 In a dry pan, toast your cumin and coriander seeds until they are coloured and release their aroma. Use a pestle and mortar or a spice grinder to grind them coarsely and tip into a bowl. Add the amchoor, salt, chilli powder and garam masala. Set aside.

5 When you are ready to cook, preheat the oven to 150°C fan/ 170°C/340°F/gas mark 3.

6 Rub the spice mix all over the pork belly. Put the bicarbonate of soda into a small bowl or mug and add the vinegar – it will fizz and foam. Use a spoon and then your fingers to spread this over the crackling.

7 Cook the pork for 2 hours. You should see the skin begin to puff up nicely. About 15 minutes before the end of the cooking time, preheat the grill (broiler) to its hottest setting. Once the 2 hours have passed, pop the pork under the grill to puff up any remaining areas of skin that have not crisped – watch carefully and keep rotating to make sure it doesn't burn. Allow to rest for 10 minutes before slicing.

butter chicken pie

There is a real trend for butter chicken these days – and when made properly I can see why everyone feels so strongly about it! It absolutely must have kasoori methi (dried fenugreek) in it, otherwise it lacks magic in my opinion. I am not here to judge, so you can make a pie with a base and lid, or you can do a pot pie, which means just topping a dish with some lovely puff pastry, eggwash, kalonji (nigella seed) and baking it.

SERVES | 4

300g (10½oz) natural (plain) yoghurt

5 tbsp tandoori masala

3 tsp ginger paste

3 tsp garlic paste

1.5kg (3lb 5oz) boneless chicken thigh (or breast), cut into 3cm (1½in) cubes

2 tbsp oil

500g (1lb 2oz) ready-made puff or shortcrust pastry (flaky pie dough)

Egg yolk, for brushing

1 tsp nigella seeds (kalonji)

SAUCE

2 tbsp ghee

2 medium white onions, finely chopped

2 tsp green chilli paste

2 tsp ginger paste

2 tsp garlic paste

500ml (2 cups) passata (strained tomatoes)

1 tsp chilli powder

2 tsp ground coriander

2 tsp ground cumin

1½ tsp garam masala

2 tsp kasoori methi (dried fenugreek)

1 tsp salt

150ml (⅔ cup) double (heavy) cream

Coriander (cilantro) leaves

1 The first job is to marinate the chicken: 24 hours is perfect but for as long as you can. Mix the yoghurt, masala, ginger and garlic pastes in a bowl and add the chicken. Cover and pop into the fridge.

2 When you are ready to cook, make the sauce. Heat the ghee in a heavy-bottomed pan, add the onions and cook for 15–20 minutes until they sweat and start to brown. Add the chilli, ginger and garlic pastes and cook for 5–6 minutes, stirring continuously. Add the passata and add 150ml (⅔ cup) water to the sauce with the ground spices and salt. Simmer for 15–20 minutes.

3 Turn your grill (broiler) to its highest setting, or you can use your oven. Take out the chicken, remove any excess marinade and put onto a baking tray greased with the oil. Grill for 15–20 minutes, turning throughout to ensure the chicken is cooked. You want to encourage colouration and a little char as it will add great flavour.

4 Finish the dish by adding the chicken to the sauce, along with the cream and a generous scattering of fresh coriander. Allow this to cool completely before making your pie. You can use shortcrust or puff pastry; my preferred version uses all-butter puff and a metal pie dish.

5 Preheat the oven to 160°C fan/180°C/375°F/gas mark 5. Line a 20cm (8in) round ovenproof dish with the rolled pastry to a thickness of about 4–5mm (¼in). Spoon in your sauce, and top with more pastry. Trim the excess (feel free to cut out shapes to decorate the top) and crimp the edges with a fork or by using your fingers and thumbs. Egg-wash the pie with a whisked yolk or two, and sprinkle with nigella seeds. Bake for 45 minutes until the filling is hot and the pastry is golden and crispy.

Masala Masters
Ruchita Green

It was a long drive to Grimsby to visit Ruchita, but my word was it worth every minute of the drive. Ruchita's mother is from Punjab and her father from Maharashtra, and she is influenced by both of these cultures in her food. On arrival, we talk about what it is like to be only one of a hundred Asian families in the area. A parallel drawn by my father as being 'like the Midlands in the 60s'. I need to touch on this because what Ruchita is doing is amazing. The infrastructure so readily available to us in the Midlands, London and across heavily diverse populated cities, is not so available in Grimsby. It took four years for Ruchita to even see anyone who wasn't white and British. Mid-Covid marked the arrival of the first local South Asian supermarket, run by a Sri Lankan couple. Until then, she would drive to Manchester, Scunthorpe or Hull to stock up on essentials. I struggle to comprehend this and immediately I am happy I bought my dad along for the journey and also grateful for the areas I have lived in and for what those communities gave us.

'My sister had come to visit from India and while we were on an escalator in a tube station in London, someone came bounding down the stairs, stopped next to me, looked me in the face and asked, "Are you from Grimsby?!"' Ruchita was, in fact, recognized by a waiter from an Indian restaurant she had visited locally at home. She tells me that there was more of a culture shock moving from Manchester to Grimsby than from Pune in India to Manchester, and I can see why she misses the multicultural joys of a big city. It is not that people are not friendly, Ruchita tells me, it's just that the community isn't established in the same way, and it makes it a little harder to celebrate your culture and make lasting relationships when there are fewer people around to do so. When my father suggests cricket as a way to get everyone together, she laughs, having just signed her son up for the Grimsby cricket club under-11s.

The main focus of her business, Masala Masters, is private parties. 'We facilitate cooking experiences in private homes, for groups of 4–12, where we cook a three-course meal together. It is usually groups of friends and family who come together for a special occasion. It is a real privilege to help celebrate their special days.' In the cookery classes Ruchita runs, almost all of her participants are English locals passionate about wanting to learn how to cook traditional Indian foods. I can't help but feel that one class at a time, step by step, she is going to make a huge difference. She designed a five-week cookery course to empower people to cook South Asian food at home and to not be afraid of spices, and along with locals wanting to join, she has also attracted interest from second-generation South Asians wanting to learn and connect with their culture through food. This is where Ruchita feels she has really won, and I agree – she is a beacon and I am not surprised people are coming to learn from her.

We cook chicken Kolhapuri together, a curry that comes from the region of Kolhapur in Maharashtra. The masala is a mixture of 15 different spices and it is typically a spicy curry packed full of flavour. 'This curry always

> In the cookery classes Ruchita runs, almost all of her participants are English locals passionate about wanting to learn how to cook traditional Indian foods.

It is difficult to contain
my excitement, as we
cook not only a dish
I have never made
before but we cook
it outside over coal
in a clay pot.

gets people interested at private nights because it is the perfect example of how complex Indian food can be, at the same time being fairly easy to bring to life', and when people have tried it they tend to get very excited. Ruchita tells me that she too first learnt to cook meat when she moved to the UK. Her friend who was homesick asked to be cooked a chicken curry instead of receiving a birthday gift and, like a great friend, Ruchita set about the task. She rang an aunt in India for the recipe, and when she asked how she might know when the chicken was cooked, her aunt replied 'it should go sort of white'. They are in fact still friends, so I think we can say the curry was a success!

It is difficult to contain my excitement, as we cook not only a dish I have never made before but we cook it outside over coal in a clay pot. As we toast spices over the charcoal and start to soften onions, I learn of Ruchita's upbringing in Pune, which she describes as 'quite a cosmopolitan city', so she also enjoys South Indian, Gujarati and Marwari food, along with a whole range of international cuisines that were available in restaurants she visited. 'I most enjoy cooking lesser known dishes from Maharashtra – they are so full of flavour and spice, and it seems a shame that there are very few opportunities for people in the UK to try them.' Ruchita is working hard to keep her culture front and centre with her in Grimsby and also keeping her children excited and engaged with that part of her heritage. Her English husband is crazy about her cooking, and the kids enjoy traditional Indian food along with all of the Western favourites (including my favourite, fish fingers).

As the onions, chilli, ginger and garlic sizzle, spices are added, along with the chicken, a little water and now it is time to wait. She tends to the fire with such skill and makes everything look totally effortless as we slowly start to smell the smoke. In the interim, just in case a whole curried chicken wasn't enough, we pop indoors to finish making some vada pav, a spicy potato mix dipped into seasoned gram flour batter before being deep-fried, served with fried green chillies and green chutney, all inside a pillowy soft white roll. It is spicy double-carb joy. 'There is a food stall halfway between Mumbai and Pune (it would mean driving about 70 miles from my hometown) that, in my opinion, serves the best vada pav. So it was a regular stop on our way to Mumbai when visiting family', and it is this vada that Ruchita wanted to recreate. While vendors may sell the same dish, there are always slight variations, and this is where you find the cult following for specific vendors and their dishes.

Hot fresh vada pav, masala tea and chicken Kolhapuri simmering over hot coals is a massive treat. When I told you it was worth the drive to Grimsby, I truly meant it. There is heart and soul in Ruchita's cooking, and you can taste it. She believes in making small adaptations, to encourage people to partake rather than to opt out if they cannot source something. But we do both wholeheartedly agree in the power of hari mirch (green finger chillies), many of which she fries for us to sandwich into our vada. It didn't take long before the chicken was cooked, and I could finally get into the pot and try it. It was remarkable. I couldn't really even draw a parallel because it was a new experience for me, but one I won't forget. The complexity of spicing, the heat from chilli, and the dimension added by cooking over fire and charcoal was incredible. Ruchita kindly packed me off with a jar full of that magical masala mix, and I vowed to buy myself a clay pot and cook in homage to her, for the most memorable lunch on a sunny day in glorious Grimbsy.

rajma, crispy roti & yoghurt

Sometimes you need recipes that are super quick and totally comforting. This is exactly that. Inexpensive, utterly delicious, vegan and a great one-pan dish that just needs a little rice or a few additional breads on the side. I really love using canned beans and pulses, not just when I'm short of time but also because they are a really good way to show your cupboard some love. I think there are times in life where you need to eat your dinner from a bowl, with a spoon, and this is perfect for those occasions.

SERVES | 2–4

2 tbsp vegetable oil

1 large white onion, chopped

2 tsp green chilli paste

2 tsp ginger paste

2 tsp garlic paste

200g (7oz/½ can) chopped tomatoes

¾ tsp ground turmeric

2 tsp ground cumin

2 tsp ground coriander

2 x 400g (14oz) cans red kidney beans

1 tsp salt

1 heaped tsp garam masala

Juice of ½ lime

Fresh coriander (cilantro), chopped

Green finger chilli, finely chopped, optional

SALSA

2 large ripe tomatoes

1 small red onion

Pinch of ground coriander

Pinch of ground sumac

Juice of 1½ limes

TO SERVE

Stale rotis, naan or flatbread

Drizzle of your preferred yoghurt

1 Begin to heat the oil in a large pan or pot, add the chopped onion and soften until translucent, about 10–12 minutes. You can get a little colour on this, don't worry. Also, we don't need the onions to cook out until super soft, because they add a great texture as we develop the dish.

2 Add the chilli, ginger and garlic pastes and cook for 6–7 minutes. Then add the tomatoes and turn up the heat. There is a particular point where the tomatoes cook out and almost split before thickening. This is what you want to happen. Add the turmeric, cumin and coriander and cook out for 5 minutes before adding the kidney beans. Turn down the heat, add the salt and about 200ml (scant 1 cup) water before simmering for about 30 minutes.

3 To make the salsa, dice your tomatoes and onion, add the coriander, sumac and lime juice and mix well. This is best left out at room temperature so it's not too cold when topping your rajma.

4 Toast your roti under the grill (broiler) or in the oven. I like to cut mine into little strips, drizzle with a little oil and bake until golden and crunchy.

5 Add the salt, garam masala and lime juice. Check the seasoning of the rajma and finish with fresh chopped coriander. If you like it a bit spicier, add a little chopped green chilli.

6 Serve the rajma in a bowl, with a drizzle of yoghurt, a spoon or two of your salsa and top with crispy roti.

malai kofta

I love malai kofta – they are obscenely good – but sometimes I find the potato a little too heavy. Here I have adapted my classic Italian gnudi recipe to create a much softer kofta, but with all the rich deliciousness of the traditional dish. For those who cannot eat potatoes, including my papa who is diabetic, this is a lovely alternative and actually isn't half as faffy as it seems. This also works really well with the coconut sauce from THAT fish curry (see page 157).

SERVES | 4

KOFTA

900g (2lb) ricotta

90g (3¼oz) finely grated (shredded) Parmesan cheese, plus extra to serve, optional

80g (2¾oz) '00' flour

2 free-range eggs, plus 1 yolk, whisked

1 tsp garam masala

½ tsp green chilli paste

Pinch of sea salt (kosher salt)

100g (3½oz) fine semolina (farina), plus extra for dusting

Olive oil, for oiling and frying

SAUCE

100ml (½ cup) extra virgin olive oil

½ tsp mustard seeds

3 fresh curry leaves

4 garlic cloves, sliced

600g (1lb 5oz) baby plum cherry tomatoes, halved

Pinch of chilli (red pepper) flakes

½ tsp garam masala

Zest of 1 unwaxed lemon and juice of ½

Fresh coriander (cilantro)

½ tsp ground cumin

½ tsp ground coriander

Sea salt and ground black pepper

1 Hang your ricotta overnight in a cheesecloth over a bowl to lose a little moisture. Then turn into a mixing bowl. Add all the other ingredients for the kofta and combine until mixed thoroughly. Roll into even lengths with a 5cm (2in) diameter dusted with a sprinkling of semolina to stop them sticking, then cut into 3–4cm (1½in) pieces. Bring a pan of salted, oiled water to the boil and blanch the kofta for 2 minutes until they float. Carefully drain onto an oiled tray.

2 To make the sauce, put your olive oil, mustard seeds, curry leaves and sliced garlic in a frying pan over a medium heat and allow to sizzle without colouring.

3 Add the tomatoes, chilli and ginger pastes, chilli flakes, garam masala, salt and black pepper to the pan and warm gently until the tomatoes start to soften and break down. Gently encourage this using the back of your wooden spoon. This sauce isn't boiled, just gently warmed because you want the tomatoes to emulsify with the oil. Add the lemon zest and juice.

4 When you are ready to eat, fry your kofta in a non-stick frying pan (skillet) with a little olive oil until golden on all sides. Put your pan-fried kofta into the sauce for 3–4 minutes, stirring carefully. Finish with additional Parmesan if you like and be sure to serve with a glass of crisp, cold white wine.

chicken & prawn kofta

Prawns give a sweetness and a juiciness to these kebabs, which I love. You can, as always, work the mix into patties for burgers or sticks like traditional kebabs. My favourite is to serve in jaldi bread with some spicy mango salad (see page 188). I might also suggest that you spread it on bread and toast it. Ciabatta works particularly well for this chicken and prawn toast version.

SERVES | 4

250g (9oz) 6% fat minced (ground) chicken

1 small bunch of spring onions (scallions), sliced and washed well

1 heaped tsp finely chopped Indian green chilli

2 tbsp ginger paste

1 tbsp garlic paste

1½ tsp garam masala

2 tsp amchoor (dried mango powder)

1 tsp ground coriander

1 tsp ground cumin

1½ tsp salt

2 small pinches of chopped fresh coriander (cilantro)

400g (14oz) raw, peeled and deveined tiger prawns (jumbo shrimp), roughly chopped

50ml (¼ cup) vegetable oil

1 Put the chicken, spring onions, ginger and garlic pastes into a large bowl. Add all the dried spices, salt and fresh coriander. Roughly chop the prawns and add to this mix. If you have a food processor, you can pop everything in at once and just pulse a couple of times to bring it all together.

2 Oil your hands using a little of the vegetable oil, then roll the mix into balls and thread onto your metal skewers. These will work well on the barbecue or under the grill (broiler), even as burger patties. Cook on a hight heat for about 10–15 minutes.

chilli prawns &
coriander polenta

I love how versatile polenta is in all its various preparations – firm, pan-fried, with obscene amounts of Parmesan and butter, with fresh herbs, roasted vegetables – all equally delicious. This is an adaptation of a shrimp and grits dish I cooked in LA. The prawns have a classic Indo-Chinese sauce and the dish is finished with a fresh salsa. It references many culinary journeys but lands squarely in a place of big flavours.

SERVES | 2–4

500g (1lb 2oz) raw, peeled and deveined tiger prawns (jumbo shrimp)

3 (bell) peppers – red, green and yellow

1 medium white onion

4 tbsp vegetable oil

1 tsp green chilli paste

1 tsp ginger paste

1 tsp garlic paste

½ tsp garam masala

2 tbsp ketchup

4 tbsp tamarind sauce

SALSA

½ bunch of spring onions (scallions), finely sliced and washed well

150g (5½oz) cherry tomatoes, quartered

Generous handful of chopped coriander (cilantro)

Pinch of salt

Juice of 1 lime, plus extra wedges to serve

2 tbsp extra virgin olive oil

POLENTA

500ml (2 cups) vegetable or chicken stock (bouillon)

120g (4¼oz) quick-cook polenta (cornmeal)

20g (¾oz) butter

Generous handful of chopped coriander (cilantro)

Salt

1 I like to split the prawns in half lengthways – this way they cook faster and the dish goes a little further. Also, when eating with a spoon (as I like to), this makes it much easier! Remove all the seeds from the peppers, then chop them and the onion to about a 1.5cm (¾in) dice. You don't have to be too disciplined with this but they need to be the same size.

2 Put all the ingredients for your salsa into a bowl and mix well.

3 Bring the stock (bouillon) to the boil in a saucepan, and season generously with salt. Tip in your polenta (cornmeal) and whisk continuously to ensure there are no lumps. Cook for 5–6 minutes until smooth and creamy.

4 Meanwhile, heat the oil in a frying pan (skillet) or wok, add the diced peppers and onion and stir-fry over a high heat, add the chilli, ginger and garlic pastes, along with the prawns (shrimp). Cook until the prawns become pink. Add the garam masala, ketchup and tamarind sauce. Mix well.

5 Finish the polenta with butter, lots of fresh coriander and add a splash of hot water if it is too firm, then check the seasoning.

6 Ladle the polenta into the middle of a bowl, spoon the prawns on top and finish with your salsa and an extra wedge of lime if you like.

spicy lamb keema lettuce cups & rice noodles

This is a really easy dish to make. I have featured it as a feast because it looks particularly special when it is put out for sharing alongside some additions from the Bits on the Side chapter. You can switch the minced (ground) lamb if that meat isn't your thing. Chicken, turkey, soy mince or even mushrooms work terrifically well. Tips: don't wear white and leave a roll of paper towel on the table because this is a get-stuck-in dish.

SERVES | 2–4

2 tbsp vegetable oil

500g (1lb 2oz) minced (ground) lamb (I like mine fairly lean) or other ground meat

1 tsp cumin seeds

2 tsp green chilli paste

2 tsp ginger paste

1 tsp garlic paste

½ tsp ground cumin

½ tsp Kashmiri chilli powder

1 tsp ground coriander

½ tsp salt

½ tsp achari masala

1 small bunch of spring onions (scallions), sliced and washed

TO SERVE

Cucumbers, cut into ribbons

Radishes, cut into wedges

Mooli (daikon), thinly sliced

Iceberg lettuce cups (cut out the root and leave upside down in a cold bowl of water: this makes it easier for you to take off the leaves)

Fresh mint

Fresh coriander (cilantro)

Chutneys

Blanched fine rice noodles, approx. 3 nests

1 Heat the oil in a wok or frying pan (skillet) and begin to brown the meat. Use a spoon to break it down and get some nice brown caramelization. Add the cumin seeds and cook for 4–5 minutes.

2 Add the chilli, ginger and garlic pastes, and cook for 3–4 minutes. Add the ground spices, salt and achaar masala along with the spring onions. Mix well and you are ready to serve!

3 I like to put some blanched rice noodles at the bottom of the lettuce cup, then top with the meat, some chutneys, fresh herbs and prepared crunchy veg, roll it up and go for it. You have to eat with your hands!

coconut curry dauphinoise

This dish is a bit of a revelation. I am sure there will be many who feel a potato gratin should accompany roast meats or feature as a side dish. But I think this is absolutely knockout. I would eat this with a green salad and a cool crisp glass of Riesling. It is vegan, it is utterly delicious and I think you may just want to make it again and again!

SERVES | 2–4

3 tbsp vegetable oil

2 large white onions, sliced as finely as possible

2 heaped tsp ginger paste

2 heaped tsp garlic paste

2 tsp green chilli paste

½ tsp ground turmeric

1 tsp garam masala

½ tsp ground cumin

½ tsp ground coriander

1 tsp salt

7 large floury (starchy) potatoes

2 cans coconut cream

300ml (1¼ cups) vegetable stock (bouillon)

1 Heat the oil in a frying pan (skillet), add the onion slices and sauté for 10 minutes or so until they soften and begin to brown. Add your pastes and cook for a further 5 minutes before adding all your spices and salt. If you need to, add a couple of tablespoons of water to make sure the spices don't burn.

2 Peel your potatoes and slice them using a mandolin if you have one, otherwise slice them as finely as you can. Aim for them to be of an even thickness otherwise the potato will not cook evenly.

3 Mix the coconut cream and stock together in a jug.

4 Preheat the oven to 180°C fan/200°C/400°F/gas mark 6. Begin to layer your potatoes in an ovenproof dish as evenly as you can. I would look to do four layers, and you want to divide your masala onion mix between these layers, finishing with a final layer of potatoes. Now pour in the coconut stock until the dish is full.

5 Bake for 1 hour or until your potatoes are tender and the dish is bubbling.

Chole Bhatture
Rajinder Kumari

I can't tell you how excited I was to meet Rajinder Auntiji. This was even before I was told about her famous chole bhatture. We met at her son Amars' house and were greeted with the type of sincere welcome that made me feel like I was visiting my own family. (Auntiji is a term of respect given amongst the South Asian community to our elders, not just those we are related to. We never refer to our elders by their first names, as a mark of respect, a pertinent cultural nuance I want to share with you.) Auntiji reminds me of my grandmother and her sisters, she is of a similar generation, and I cannot help but think of all the wonderful conversations about pind (village), sabjis and life they would have had together, but also how lucky I was to be having them myself.

Auntiji came to the UK in the late 1960s and life began in Aston, Birmingham with her family. A move to London saw them start a grocery shop business in Hounslow. Once married, Auntiji tells me, 'We came, there was no problem for us as we had our own house, we lived together as a big family and we already knew where to shop and what we needed to buy to cook for ourselves.' The community that had established itself in London was growing and was welcoming to the entrepreneurial talents of the South Asian community. I become aware that I was speaking to someone who has been an integral part of the establishment of our community and the infrastructure of goods needed to support it. To some, this may be a fairly normal conversation about family history, and a story of immigration and settling that is perfectly ordinary, because we have heard them frequently. But in exploring my own

family stories, I encourage you to look at your own. There is a tendency within immigrant communities to take a lot in their stride and phrases like 'it's how it was' and 'we did what we needed to' don't convey the magnitude of their bravery or their grit. It's also very easy not to take time to relate to the struggles of those who paved the way for us, because things may be a little easier for us. Let us take a moment to show gratitude to all of the auntijis and unclejis who started businesses and to all those who worked in them. The foundations for our lives now were laid back then: something to consider when you need curry leaves and fenugreek at 10 o'clock at night. These stories are not ordinary. They are remarkable. And while the people telling them often don't acknowledge or accept their achievements and value, we should be thanking them anyway.

For Auntiji, cooking at home was not dissimilar to the way she cooked in India. 'We used to go to local Pakistani shops that would sell all that we needed to cook at home. We never wasted anything; we would use leftover dhal to make dhal parantha and kadi when the yoghurt was slightly sour – all traditional ways to cook, ways we have cooked always.' Zero waste, farm-to-fork cooking has been done across the world, by so cultures and unsurprisingly it starts at home. After grocery stores, Auntiji, along with her husband, took on a dry cleaners – but not just any dry cleaners: whatever food was prepared at home was brought to the shop. 'Our customers became our family and friends; samosas, sabjis, pakoras, whatever we made we would take to share', ultimately building and caring for a community through food.

> In 50 years – we haven't ordered in a pizza or takeaway because we love our home food so much.

"

It is so important to me that I cook traditional food, that my children enjoy it and so do my grandchildren.

'In 50 years – we haven't ordered in pizza or takeaway because we love our home food so much,' I am told. And frankly after one bite of her bhattura, it's blindingly obvious why. Auntiji loves to cook traditional Punjabi food, 'food from home'. Once upon a time, I eye-rolled at the idea of daily Indian food, being told by both my parents that 'one day, you'll understand', and now, hand on heart, I do. Food maintains identity, culture and community and being so very far from home, it has no doubt helped prevent both Auntiji and Uncleji from feeling too homesick, something to comfort and take the edge off a little, after such huge life-changing moves.

Auntiji has the most wonderful energy. She beams and smiles continuously and in turn so do I! She laughs, makes me laugh and there is a little moment where I think if I had been born a little earlier, I may have had a little more time like this with my own grandmother. She operates like a General in her directives to her family to start preparing the table for lunch. Both Uncleji and Amars operate with speed and smiles, and also a knowledge that this lady is a real force of nature – those smiles are of pride and gratitude. I am shown a jar full of garam masala, that naturally is homemade to a blend specific to Auntiji's likes. The aroma is magnificent. Individual spices are purchased, roasted and blitzed into a sublime, personal seasoning across all food, something that has been perfected over many decades of learning and no doubt bequeathed via that special 'osmosis' of handing-down learning.

Not only as Auntiji, but also as a Biji (grandmother) to two gorgeous children, I am told, 'It is so important to me that I cook traditional food, that my children enjoy it and so do my grandchildren.' We talk about ingredients and I am duly informed that they do not need to be expensive but 'with the right ingredients you can make something very special'. Auntiji and Uncleji grow their own vegetables and herbs in their garden. Marrows, tomatoes, beans, onions, saag (greens) – 'we know how to grow vegetables, we are Punjabi!' And out comes a cheeky giggle from us both. When asked what is important, we land on the magic of chilli. 'You cannot make proper Indian food without green finger chillies' – they add heat but they also add flavour. If you have ever had to make a traditional Indian dish without hari mirch (green finger chillies) and wondered what wasn't quite right about it, then it was probably this it lacked. The next jar of joy I am shown is fenugreek, homed in a repurposed peanut butter jar (see, zero waste). 'We grow our own methi, I dry it out and then use it for the whole year in my cooking.' The aroma is incredible, an elite level of methi.

We were going to cook chole together, but Auntiji runs such a tight ship, she had cooked everything already so we could just chat and enjoy lunch. Chickpeas (garbanzo beans) are washed three times, soaked for 24 hours in cold water with a little bicarbonate of soda (baking soda). They are boiled and pressure-cooked for an hour. We then make the masala with

ginger, chilli, garlic, tomato, onions and plenty of that homemade garam masala – 'you can't find this in the shops!' We reheat the bhatture and make a little salad, where I witness again the universal skill of chopping onto your thumb that I know and love so well.

'I am vegetarian, so all of the food we eat is vegetarian, but I do sometimes make chicken for the children. I don't feel like we need to eat meat when there are so many delicious vegetables and dhals to eat.' It seems clear to me that the clean-eating, zero waste, farm-to-fork, no single-use plastic lifestyle that is popular now has been here all along. Auntiji's grandchildren are now also the third-culture crew, and lucky enough to celebrate their mixed heritage of English and South Asian backgrounds. 'Our culture lives through our food. This is how my grandchildren can enjoy our culture, it is different for them, but I want them to be excited by our food just like my daughter-in-law is. I taught her to make dhal and aloo gobi and her food is delicious, I am so glad they can all enjoy this.' Everything done is done for the family, with love and, from the way Auntiji speaks, you can feel this. 'My husband helps me cook at home, we do everything together: growing, cooking and, of course, the eating!' What a dream team they make!

We sit for lunch, chatting, laughing and sharing. We serve each other, passing things around the table, making sure everyone has a little of everything before offering yet more. I eat my chole bhattura, with my hands, sat next to Auntiji, who interrupts her own lunch only to serve more food onto my plate, and encourage others to eat some more. When I tell her how utterly delicious the food is, she beams. 'Every day I cook, I can cook something different – and if you don't enjoy your food, you don't feel happy!' Three bhatture and two helpings of chole later, I can confirm I feel very happy!

ox cheek masala, pickled shallots & coriander sauce vierge

This is a super-rich, delicious curry, heady with black cardamom and sweet with soft roasted onions. Like most deep, rich braises, it is always really lovely to have something to cut the richness – and this for me is in the form of a coriander sauce vierge and some simply pickled shallots. Serve with rice, spicy crushed potatoes (see page 186) or some naan. You can also break the meat down and eat it as you would a taco, on some lovely naan. This tastes even better the next day, or even the day after, as most curries do. This isn't something to be made in a rush, it's a labour of love, time and attention – and is so worth it.

SERVES | 4

2 ox cheeks, trimmed of fat and sinew

5 tbsp vegetable oil

2 large white onions, chopped then blended to a purée

1 tsp black cumin seeds

6 fresh curry leaves

3 tsp ginger paste

3 tsp green chilli paste

4 tsp garlic paste

250ml (generous 1 cup) passata (strained tomatoes)

1 tsp ground turmeric

1 tsp ground cumin

1 tsp ground coriander

1 tsp Kashmiri chilli powder

2 black cardamom pods

3 green cardamom pods

1 cassia bark or cinnamon stick

2 tbsp tamarind sauce

½ tsp ground black pepper

1½ tsp salt

1 medium red onion

3 tablespoons white wine vinegar

Crispy shallots/onions, to serve

1 Cut the ox cheeks into 2–4 pieces, depending on size.

2 Heat the oil in a large heavy-bottomed or cast-iron pan, add the onions and cook over a medium heat for about 20–30 minutes. This does take time, but what is 30 minutes in the scheme of culinary magic?

3 Turn up the heat and add the cumin seeds, curry leaves and the ginger, chilli and garlic pastes. Add the ox cheeks at this point. Cook, stirring vigorously, before adding your passata and the remaining spices and salt.

4 At this point, add 250ml (1 cup) water and reduce the heat to a slow blip. You can let this simmer on the hob (stove top), but I like to put the lid on my cast-iron pan and pop it in the oven for about 4–5 hours at 150°C fan/170°C/325°F/gas mark 3.

5 Meanwhile, finely slice the red onion, put in a small bowl and pour over the white vinegar. I prefer not to warm my vinegar or add sugar as I like the onions to retain their crunch and be quite punchy with acidity. Set aside until you are ready to serve.

Continued overleaf

ox cheek masala, pickled shallots & coriander sauce vierge *continued*

SAUCE VIERGE

2 large ripe tomatoes, deseeded and diced

4 spring onions (scallions), washed and finely chopped

2 generous pinches of fresh coriander leaves, plus extra to serve (use the stalks too)

¼ tsp green chilli paste

Zest of 1 unwaxed lemon and juice of ½

6 To make the sauce vierge, finely dice your tomatoes after removing the seeds and pop into a bowl. Add the spring onions, chopped coriander stalks and leaves, lemon zest and juice, finishing with the green chilli paste. I like to blend all the ingredients (except the tomato) in a little chopper, then stir through the diced tomato; this creates a lovely vibrant sauce.

7 Check the seasoning of your ox cheeks and add a little more salt if needed. After a long time cooking, the sauce should be rich, dark and full of flavour, with the meat soft, yielding and utterly delicious. Serve by plating if you wish but, for me, feasting is about sharing. So, scatter the pickled red onion slices over the ox cheeks, along with a drizzle of vierge, some crispy shallots and fresh coriander leaves – with more vierge to serve at the table.

THAT fish curry

As some of you may know – I did have a little play on *Great British Menu*, and on my first year I cooked a fish curry for Daniel Clifford. He cried, I cried – we all cried and I got a 10. It was a wonderful moment. Fast forward to the following year – I rather controversially (who, me???) made the same dish for Paul Ainsworth – and would you believe, it got another 10. I have lost track of how many times I have been asked for this recipe. If you cannot get the crab, don't worry, just don't put it in, I promise it will be equally delicious, and if you want to add a bit of extra oomph, pop in some tiger prawns (jumbo shrimp). Equally, the base of this recipe is purely vegan, so you can drop in vegetables you love, or some soft-boiled eggs.

SERVES | 4

400g (14oz) monkfish tails, cut into 2.5cm (1in) cubes, or whatever fish you like, skinned and deboned

MARINADE

2 tbsp vegetable oil

1 tsp green chilli paste

2 tsp ginger paste

¼ bunch of coriander (cilantro)

1 tsp chilli powder

2 tsp amchoor (dried mango powder)

½ tsp salt

1 First make the marinade. Put all the ingredients into a little blender and whizz up. Pour over the monkfish and allow to marinate overnight or for at least a couple of hours.

2 To make the curry (see ingredients overleaf), heat the oil in a large pot or pan. Add the mustard seeds, curry leaves and dried red chillies. Sizzle to release the aromas before adding the onions. Cook for about 20–25 minutes over a medium heat, stirring well to make sure it doesn't catch.

3 Add the chilli and ginger and garlic pastes and cook for 5–6 minutes.

4 Add the passata and cook for 12–15 minutes until it splits.

5 Add the turmeric, cumin, ground coriander, cooking for a moment before adding the coconut milk. Reduce the heat, allow to simmer for 5–10 minutes before adding the brown crab meat.

6 Add the monkfish and cook for another 8–10 minutes or so. Finish the dish with the fresh white crab, lime juice, garam masala and fresh coriander. Serve with rice, breads – anything you like.

Continued overleaf

THAT fish curry *continued*

CURRY

100ml (scant ½ cup) mustard oil

2 tbsp black mustard seeds

3 curry leaves

2 dried red chillies, left whole

1 large white onion, chopped or blended into a purée

1 tsp chopped green finger chilli

2 tsp ginger paste

1 tsp garlic paste

200ml (scant 1 cup) passata (strained tomatoes)

1 tbsp ground turmeric

1 tsp ground cumin

1 tsp ground coriander

500ml (2 cups) coconut milk

Juice of 1 lime

200g (7oz) brown crab meat

450g (1lb) handpicked white crab meat

Juice of 1 big lime

2 tsp garam masala

Fresh coriander (cilantro), to finish

Note: Monkfish holds itself together in this recipe, but if you are using salmon or another flaky fish, first stir in the white crab meat, lime juice, garam masala and fresh coriander before adding your fish, to avoid breaking up your fish.

whole roasted Chettinad duck

It isn't often that I cook duck – but when I do, I like to roast the whole bird over a low heat, then turn up the oven to get a nice crispy skin. There is no reason why you can't eat this with tamarind chutney, roomali roti, and parathas with cucumber and spring onions. Or serve it as the jewel of your Sunday lunch. It makes remarkable leftover sandwiches, quesadillas and is delicious in salads. This spice mix, once made, can also be used with the same method for slow-cooked pork belly (see page 130), or even on squash salad (see page 99). The duck will benefit from drying out in the fridge, uncovered, for a day or so before you are ready to cook.

SERVES | 4

1 medium duck (approx. 1.8kg/4lb)

Salt

Tamarind sauce

CHETTINAD SPICE MIX

12 black peppercorns

6cm (2½in) cinnamon stick

10 dried red chillies

2 star anise

2 tsp cumin seeds

1 tsp ajwain (carom) seeds

5 green cardamom pods

2 tsp fennel seeds

4 tsp coriander seeds

7 cloves

2 dried curry leaves

2 tsp poppy seeds

½ tsp fenugreek seeds

2 mace blades

1 Pop all the spice mix ingredients into a dry frying pan (skillet) over a medium heat for about 10 minutes until the aromas are released and they are well toasted. You may need to gently shake the pan to ensure they toast evenly.

2 Allow to cool and blend in a spice grinder – in a nice airtight container this mix will last well in your cupboard.

3 Preheat the oven to 150°C fan/170°C/325°F/gas mark 3. Gently score your duck with a sharp knife. You absolutely do not want to cut through the skin to the flesh, so gentle scoring is recommended.

4 Rub the duck with 3 tablespoons of your Chettinad spice mix and a pinch of salt.

5 Place the duck in a roasting tin (pan) and roast for 3–3½ hours, draining out the rendered fat from time to time. I would suggest roasting some par-boiled potatoes in the fat to serve alongside.

6 Check the duck towards the end of the cooking time: it should be golden, burnished and getting crispy. Brush the duck with the tamarind sauce and turn up the heat to 200°C fan/220°C/425°F/gas mark 7 for the last 15 minutes.

7 Allow the bird to rest for 10 minutes and carve or shred the meat.

jaggery roasted ham, egg & chips

I am not even a little sorry to announce my love for ham, egg and chips (French fries). When we visited Lambra – the pind (village) where my grandparents lived in Punjab – my grandmother would make us homemade chips that we would eat with ketchup which my grandfather had safely brought back from the UK. A tiny pinch of garam masala and salt made them tremendously moreish. There is something so beautiful in how joyously nostalgic and simple this dish is and we haven't even got to the leftover ham sandwich with slaw yet! You don't have to do this with eggs and chips – of course it can become your Christmas ham or even an alternative Sunday lunch.

SERVES | 4

1kg (2lb 4oz) unsmoked gammon joint

2 small onions

2 bay leaves

4 black peppercorns

5cm (2in) piece of fresh ginger

1 cinnamon stick

GLAZE

60g (2¼oz) jaggery

8 tbsp tamarind (imli) sauce, plus extra to serve

3 tsp ginger paste

1 tsp green chilli paste (if you like)

½ tsp ground black cardamom

½ tsp ground black pepper

CHIPS

6 large floury (starchy) potatoes

Salt

½ tsp garam masala or chaat masala

Vegetable oil

1 I like to soak the gammon in water for a couple of hours. Then put it into a pan of fresh cold water with all the aromatics. Bring to the boil, then turn down to a simmer, cooking for 45 minutes to 1 hour.

2 Meanwhile, pop all the glaze ingredients into another pan and melt gently before removing from the heat. Preheat the oven to 180°C fan/200°C/400°F/gas mark 6.

3 Carefully pull off the skin from the ham and discard it. Put the ham into a roasting dish or ovenproof dish, pour over half the glaze and roast for about 15 minutes. Add the remainder of the glaze and roast for another 15 minutes before removing and resting.

4 Peel your potatoes and cut into 1.5cm (⅝in) chips (French fries). Rinse in cold water and dry on paper towel. Pop into a bowl, season with the salt, masala and oil and mix well. I like to cook mine on a baking sheet lined with baking paper so they don't stick. Lay them out and cook in the preheated oven for about 50 minutes. You will need to turn the chips to make sure they cook evenly.

5 Serve with fried eggs and a little more tamarind sauce.

roasted squash orzotto, crispy onions & ginger

You can use leftover basmati to make khichidi for this, but I have always really loved the way orzo retains its shape and texture. It's such a versatile ingredient, and it always seems to be left in the back of the cupboard after being used only once – often for a salad. The richness and creaminess of this dish comes from the squash and onions. The dish is vegan – but you can, should you fancy, add a little tarka with some butter for richness.

SERVES | 2

1 small butternut squash

1 large white onion, sliced

3 tbsp vegetable oil

1 tsp ground cumin

1 tsp ground coriander

1 tsp coriander seeds

300g (10½oz) orzo

Crispy shallots/onions

Fresh coriander (cilantro), to garnish

TEMPERED SPICES

2 tbsp vegetable oil

3 curry leaves

1 tsp garlic paste

1 tsp ginger paste

1 tsp cumin seeds

Thumb-sized piece of fresh ginger, julienned

½ tsp garam masala

Salt

1 Preheat the oven to 180°C fan/200°C/400°F/gas mark 6. Peel the squash, halve, remove the seeds and cut into and cut it into 1cm (½in) cubes. Spread the squash over a baking tray along with the onion slices. Sprinkle with the oil, salt, ground cumin, ground coriander and coriander seeds and roast for 20 minutes until soft.

2 Meanwhile, cook your orzo following the packet instructions, usually for about 8–10 minutes. You don't want it to be overcooked, so try to retain some bite by cooking for 2 minutes less than suggested.

3 When your roasted squash wedges and onion slices are soft, pop them into a blender with a splash of the cooking water from the orzo. You should be able to blend this into a smooth sauce.

4 For the tempered spices, add all the ingredients to a small frying pan over a medium heat and fry until the curry leaves are crispy and the garlic's aroma is released.

5 Drain the orzo and return to the saucepan. Stir in the squash sauce and garnish with the tempered spices, crispy shallots and fresh coriander.

Bits on the Side

Additional treats to turn
meals into feasts and to
create opportunities for
you to mix and match
your dishes. Absolutely
never an afterthought,
bits on the side bring
extra flavour, texture and
interest to what is already
on the table.

Growing up, there were always amazing additions arriving on the table to go with whichever delicious dishes had just been prepared. Parathas would be accompanied by yoghurt and achaar, kebabs served with homemade green chutney, and almost everything came with butter (!), or a lovely bowl of fresh crunchy mooli (daikon), seasoned with lemon and black salt. The table would be full of little plates of this and that, with everything holding its own as far as flavour went.

I confess that I get as equally excited about sides as I do main dishes. I have always been this way – and, as with most things I can't explain, I just put it down to my Punjabi appetite. Some of these dishes take a little effort and then become part of the kitchen pyar so you will have them on hand, ready to jazz up anything you are cooking; others need to be made fresh and enjoyed there and then.

Breads, chutneys, pickles, butters, salads, potatoes – they are all here for you to play around with. The aim was to create a collection of recipes with plenty of flexibility that would allow you to decide which main dishes you might assign them to. As ever, there are no hard and fast rules; these are recipes for you to enjoy adapting.

no-yeast naan

When you want to have naan but you don't want to wait for dough to prove, this is the recipe for you. Obviously you don't get quite the same amount of aeration in the dough for those gorgeous burnished bubbles but it's pretty great and nice and soft. You don't have to use the grill (broiler) but it mimics the tandoor if used on its highest setting.

MAKES 4–5 NAAN

300g (10½oz) self-raising (self-rising) flour, plus extra for rolling

½ tsp baking powder

½ tsp salt

300g (10½oz) Greek-style yoghurt, or vegan yoghurt works nicely too

2 tbsp vegetable oil, plus extra for brushing

OPTIONS

Ghee, butter or spiced butter (see page 184), for brushing

½ tsp nigella seeds (kalonji)

Chopped coriander (cilantro)

1 Sift your flour and baking powder into a bowl, add the salt and yoghurt and mix with a knife to bring everything together. You don't really want to knead this, keep a light touch. When your dough is mixed, oil your hands and pour the remainder of the oil into the dough. Shape into a nice ball and leave for 20 minutes somewhere warmish. Roll into balls using a little more flour if you need to and roll out into rounds about 5mm (⅛in) thick, or a little thicker if you prefer.

2 Heat a tawa, heavy-bottomed frying pan or a cast-iron skillet over a medium heat and pop a naan on it. If it's a ridged skillet, you can turn it when the bar ridge marks are made and then finish with oil, ghee or butter. If using a tawa or frying pan, you will need to preheat the grill (broiler) to hot. Put the naan in the pan until you see it begin to bubble: at this point pop it under the hot grill and watch more bubbles form. You can colour the naan as much as you want before brushing it with oil, ghee or butter.

Tunworth cheese naan

Now, this is one of those dishes that for me typically highlights the magic of culture clashing. I love, love, LOVE Tunworth cheese. Of course, you can use any soft camembert-style cheese you like but, for me, a Tunworth is a treat and while there isn't often much left from the cheeseboard, when there is this is a really delicious way to use it up.

MAKES 4–5 NAAN

300g (10½oz) self-raising (self-rising) flour, plus extra for rolling

½ tsp baking powder

½ tsp salt

300g (10½oz) Greek-style yoghurt

2 tbsp vegetable oil

1 Tunworth or 250g (9oz) other camembert-style cheese, at room temperature

1 tsp nigella seeds (kalonji)

OPTIONS

A little chopped Indian green chilli or amchoor onions (see page 184)

Oil, ghee or butter, for brushing

1 Sift your flour and baking powder into a bowl, add the salt and yoghurt and mix with a knife to bring everything together. You don't really want to knead this, keep a light touch. When your dough is mixed, oil your hands and pour the remainder of the oil into the dough. Shape into a nice ball and leave for 20 minutes somewhere warmish. Roll into balls using a little more flour if you need to and roll out into rounds about 5mm (⅛in) thick, or a little thicker if you prefer.

2 Take a generous slice of Tunworth, add a little green chilli, if you like, or amchoor onions and pop into the middle, fold up the sides around the cheese and pinch to ensure the dough is closed. Lightly flour and then roll out as you normally would. It's important the cheese is at room temperature here otherwise it will be a little tricky to roll.

3 Heat a tawa, heavy-bottomed frying pan or a cast-iron skillet over a medium heat and pop a naan on it. If it's a ridged skillet, you can turn it when the bar marks are made and then finish with oil, ghee or butter. If using a tawa or frying pan, you will need to preheat the grill (broiler) to hot. Put the naan in the pan until you see it begin to bubble: at this point pop it under the hot grill and watch more bubbles form. You can colour the naan as much as you want before brushing it with oil, ghee or butter.

coconut naan

I do know a few people who really enjoy the combination of sweeter breads with hotter curries. I have always loved coconut but the addition of toasting it prior to making the naan makes it a bit special.

MAKES 4–5 NAAN

60g (2¼oz) desiccated (shredded) coconut

300g (10½oz) self-raising (self-rising) flour

½ tsp baking powder

½ tsp salt

¼ tsp caster (superfine) sugar

300g (10½oz) coconut yoghurt

2 tbsp vegetable or coconut oil

1 Pop your desiccated (shredded) coconut into a dry frying pan (skillet) and toast gently for 4–5 minutes over a medium heat. You need to keep gently shaking the pan to ensure it doesn't burn. You should see a lovely gentle golden colour and your kitchen should begin to smell deliciously of coconut.

2 Follow the method for no-yeast naan on page 168.

jaldi bread

This soft wheat bread is known as jaldi because it can be made very quickly – that's what the word means. I think it's good to have a couple of great easy flatbread recipes on hand because frankly the time needed for dough to prove and double rise isn't always available. This is even faster if you have a mixer with a dough hook. You can use a food processor but pulse rather than blitz the ingredients together, then let it rest for twice the stated time.

MAKES 8–10 FLATBREADS

200g (7oz) plain (all-purpose) flour, plus extra for rolling

¾ tsp baking powder

½ tsp fine salt

5 tbsp vegetable oil

125ml (½ cup) warm water

1 Sift the dry ingredients into the bowl of your mixer fitted with a dough hook and turn on, add the oil to the warm water and slowly drizzle in. Mix for 2 minutes until a smooth ball of dough has formed. Roll into 8–10 balls and allow the dough to rest for 20 minutes. Usually if it hasn't rested the dough will contract as you try to roll it – so the resting is very important.

2 Dip each ball into a little extra flour and roll to an even thickness of 3–4mm (⅛in). This means not only will they cook quickly but they also won't be brittle. Cook on a tawa for 20 seconds on each side and then stack one on top of the other – the heat and moisture will keep them soft.

fresh green chutney

Coriander and mint chutney and cheese toasties (grilled cheese sandwiches) made in a toastie machine is a joyful memory for me. There isn't really anything that this chutney doesn't work with. You can also fold it through a little plain yoghurt and use it as a marinade or a dip.

MAKES ENOUGH FOR A JAM JAR

2 thumb-sized pieces of fresh ginger, peeled

2 fat garlic cloves

1 small bunch of mint leaves

½ small bunch of coriander (cilantro)

½ tsp salt

4 green finger chillies

1 heaped tsp amchoor (dried mango powder)

2 tbsp water

5 tbsp rice wine vinegar

1 Pop everything into a blender and blitz. Taste and feel free to add a little more salt or chilli.

EATING

With kebabs, as a marinade or with any type of grilled cheese!

Biji's chutney 1967

There may be times when you can't get your hands on imli chutney – it was the same for my grandma in the 60s. Biji would make samosas and kebabs upstairs at The Ash Tree pub, destined for sale on the bar downstairs. At a time where it was tricky to get hold of specialist South Asian ingredients it was imperative to be creative in trying to replicate flavours from home. And so... Biji's chutney was born, using a readily available items from most shops that sat proudly next to samosas, pakoras and shami kebabs. I am informed by my father, who would pull pints behind the bar – that even if the snacks had sold out, it wasn't uncommon for people to ask for the chutney anyway, just so they could get a little taster of a more familiar and beloved flavour from home.

MAKES | ENOUGH FOR 2

5 tbsp ketchup

5 tsbp brown sauce

1 tbsp mint sauce

Pinch of salt

Pinch of sugar

Pinch of garam masala

2 tbsp water

1 I hope you're ready for how difficult this is. Pop everything in the bowl, mix and serve.

roasted onion & chilli chutney

This is a punchy chutney, one that can be made at the same time you are doing a barbecue, or prepped in the oven. Either way, do make absolutely sure you get that well-done char across all the vegetables – it creates a super flavour.

MAKES ENOUGH FOR A JAM JAR OF GOODNESS

1 large white onion, roughly cut into large chunks

4 fat garlic cloves

3 ripe small tomatoes, halved

1 red (bell) pepper, cut into eighths, seeds removed

Thumb-sized piece of fresh ginger, peeled and roughly chopped

3 green finger chillies

5 tbsp rapeseed (canola) oil

1 tsp salt

1 tsp black cumin seeds

½ small bunch of fresh coriander (cilantro)

Juice of 1 lime

1 Preheat the oven to 190°C fan/210°C/410°F/gas mark 6½. Put the onion, garlic, tomatoes, pepper, ginger and chillies on a baking tray or in a large oven dish. Ideally they will be nicely spread out so that they can char properly. Drizzle with the oil, scatter over the salt and cumin and mix well.

2 Roast for about 20–25 minutes, turning the veg once or twice to ensure even colouring.

3 When everything is burnished and coloured nicely, remove from the oven and allow to rest for 10 minutes.

4 Pop into a blender along with the coriander and lime juice. Blitz while warm until smooth. Check for salt and adjust if needed.

EATING

Super delicious with kebabs, roast chicken, or with tortilla chips.

Make a cheese toastie (grilled cheese sandwich) with a smear of this chutney for a serious power up.

kasundi tomato relish

This is another one of those items that you should commit to making once a month to give you a mammoth flavour reward on days you're not feeling like having a big cook. Use cherry tomatoes, overripe tomatoes, tomatoes in the reduced aisle at the supermarket and, if you want, you can use a can of chopped tomatoes instead. An instant level up on your cheese on toast, scrambled eggs, waffles, kebabs or simply on fresh bread.

**MAKES ENOUGH FOR
2 JAM JARS**

3 tbsp vegetable oil

1 tsp mustard seeds

½ tsp cumin seeds

½ tsp fennel seeds

½ tsp coriander seeds

1 large white onion, finely sliced

2 tbsp ginger paste

2 tsp green chilli paste

3 garlic cloves

½ tsp Kashmiri chilli powder

½ tsp ground turmeric

7 medium tomatoes or 500g
(1lb 2oz) cherry tomatoes,
roughly chopped

3 tbsp muscovado (soft dark brown)
sugar

100ml (scant ½ cup) vinegar,
white or red

½ tsp nigella seeds (kalonji)

1 tsp sea salt

1 Heat the oil in a heavy-bottomed saucepan over a medium heat. Add all the seeds and allow them to start to sizzle in the oil before adding the onion, the ginger and chilli pastes and garlic. Cook for about 8–10 minutes, then stir in the Kashmiri chilli powder and turmeric.

2 Add the tomatoes and increase the heat a little. Pop a lid on for 3–4 minutes until the tomatoes begin to break down. Add the sugar, vinegar, nigella seeds and salt and turn the heat to low. Stir well and let this cook for about 15 minutes, uncovered. The vinegar and sugar will reduce the tomatoes to create a delicious chutney.

3 Pour into sterilized jars or a clean airtight container and eat with everything.

achaari mayonnaise

So this is a bit of a revelation. This couldn't be simpler to make but it really is perfect with just about everything. Initially I made it as a dip for crispy squid but I ended up trying it with various leftovers – to absolute triumph. Two ingredients, one of which you can swap out to make it totally vegan. Winning. You will need a blender, or a little chopper. If you don't have either, I suggest you just chop the achaar as finely as you can and hand mix.

Now, achaar isn't like a chutney. It is a heady savoury, spicy, delicious pickle whereby fruits and vegetables retain their crunch and yield to their preservation all at the same time. You can use whichever types of pickle you have: lime, lemon, ginger, even green chilli if you like. Just be careful of stones when you blend or chop.

MAKES ENOUGH FOR A JAM JAR

140g (5oz) mayo (vegan mayo if you like)

4 tbsp mango and ginger achaar (or any pickle you like)

1 Pop the mayo and pickle into a little chopper and blend. Store in a sterilized jar or clean airtight container.

'vinegar' for your fried bits

As a stickler for acidity in almost all food, I love the way it cuts through and provides freshness. I think this stems from the eye-watering amounts of vinegar I liked to put on my chips (French fries) as a child (I still do!). This is a kind of seasoned savoury vinegar that you can use as you would malt vinegar on tasty fried items like fish pakoras, crispy squid or even your chips.

MAKES ENOUGH FOR A LITTLE JAM JAR

40ml (1¼fl oz) malt vinegar

40ml (1¼fl oz) white wine vinegar

¼ tsp amchoor (dried mango powder)

½ tsp Kashmiri chilli powder

½ tsp ground cumin

¼ tsp salt

1 Put all the ingredients in a clean jam jar, seal and shake it well. If you can, reuse an old vinegar bottle, then it's perfect for shaking over your hot fried goodies.

curry leaf & crispy garlic chilli oil

My love for chilli is profound. It doesn't always have to be the type of heat that causes perspiration – but it really can help even the simplest item become just a little more interesting. This is variant of all of those incredible Chinese crispy chilli oils (that my fridge is also full of!). I thought it would be great to create one that had spices aligned to those you might have in your cupboards anyway – and also a good way to use up any fresh curry leaves that you perhaps didn't manage to freeze in time. The MSG here is optional – so as you please.

MAKES A BIG JARFUL

120ml (½ cup) vegetable oil

2 banana shallots, finely sliced

8 garlic cloves, finely sliced

1 tsp black peppercorns

Thumb-sized piece of fresh ginger, peeled and chopped finely

30g chilli (red pepper) flakes

2 star anise

1 cassia bark stick

1 tsp ajwain (carom) seeds

1 tsp cumin seeds

1 tsp coriander seeds

10 small fresh curry leaves

4 mace blades

1 tsp grated jaggery (or brown sugar)

1 Pop the veg oil into a saucepan, add the finely sliced shallots, sliced garlic, peppercorns, ginger, chilli flakes, star anise and cassia bark and bring to a gentle sizzle. Cook for about 20 minutes over a medium–low heat. Check carefully how crispy all your bits are getting and, when you are almost there, add the ajwain, cumin and coriander seeds, curry leaves and mace. Be careful when you add the curry leaves – they may cause a little crackle in the oil. Cook for a further 2–3 minutes. Store in a sterilized jar.

Cue Point
Mursal Saiq

I have wanted to meet Mursal for a very long time. And when she said yes to cooking with me and being involved in my book, I was really thrilled. She is co-founder of Cue Point, a social enterprise food business that includes residencies, but also goes on tour with various food festivals. She and her partner Joshua specialize in British Afghan BBQ with the tagline 'bbq for the many not the few'. It's an outlet for abundant creativity but also in her words, 'the merging of our British heritage, ethnic backgrounds and personal experiences of growing up in London'. She too operates in the third-kid culture technicolour realm, and she is extremely vocal about inclusivity, accessibility and representation – I am here for it. I was lucky enough to spend a morning cooking at her family home with her and her mother Zohra Aunty and to have a wonderful garden tour with her father Abdul Uncle.

Mursal's mother Zohra Aunty was a science and maths teacher at university in Afghanistan, prior to one of the first Taliban uprisings in the 1990s. When schools were forced to close and education ground to a halt, she was unable to work as all teachers and students were made to stay at home. She and her husband moved to Mumbai to live for a while before coming to the UK. Zohra Aunty tells me she loved India, and would like to revisit, before reeling off a list of familiar markets, shops and squares she enjoyed visiting when she resided there. Mursal says, 'I remember my time in India well – Holi festival, drawing princesses in my workbooks at school', these memories have stuck with her, perhaps a little more than her memories of Afghanistan she admits. 'In India, I got to be free.'

Mursal studied history and political philosophy and her core ethos is about integration, which works hand in hand with immigration, and this Mursal delivers through the medium of food, by having some very frank conversations and by enrolling people to acknowledge how much they don't know. Admitting this is a good start before you begin working with her, and I love her brutal honesty. Racial equity, creating safe spaces, saying no to 'cancel culture'. She has real first-hand experience that has shaped her, but she feels a lot of this is owed to residing in Hackney. When the Saiqs arrived in the UK, they lived in North London, and this was neither warm nor welcoming for them. A number of unpleasant encounters led her father to ask 'where the most refugees were', and the family moved to Hackney.

Mursal smiles broadly when telling me what this move was like for her, and attributes much of who she is and how she has grown to the multicultural magic of the area. 'Hackney is a hub of diversity and the immigrant community; diversity brings confidence, it brings innovation, it does so much.' This confidence enables her to speak out and oppose gentrification in areas that have been home to many different cultures, and defend spaces that rightfully belong to those nurturing and developing them. Her new school hosted something called World Food Day – Somali, Pakistani, Bangladeshi, Nigerian, Yemeni, Croatian, Afghan families and food – 'nobody spoke particularly good English, but you really didn't need to. We smiled, we shared and that was that. We felt so accepted'. After hearing some of her stories, I can only imagine her joy at finally having a place where she was welcome.

"

Hackney is a hub
of diversity and the
immigrant community;
diversity brings confidence,
it brings innovation, it
does so much.

> On the one occasion Mursal was able to travel back to Afghanistan, she told me that she tangibly noticed the fact she was a 'diasporic kid', not totally Afghan, and yet not totally British.

We are cooking borani banjan with Zohra Aunty. This is a traditional Afghani aubergine dish made with fried aubergine, garlic yoghurt, a spicy tomato sauce and finished with fresh mint. It is epic. Zohra Aunty peels her aubergines, before salting and cooking, but in Mursal's British–Afghan version she doesn't. Her mum shakes her head in disapproval about aubergine-gate, but smiles when Mursal says 'it's British Afghan, Mummy!' I love this real-time evolution but also understand that when you're catering for some pretty huge events like Mursal does, peeling aubergines is a lot to do.

We fry them, chopping garlic, tomatoes from the garden, a little chilli and some light spice. I see Mursal keen to use some green chilli, me happy to and Aunty Zohra being mindful we don't add too much. The onion, chilli and garlic sauce is cooked down with a few spices and left to simmer while the other elements are prepared. Already the kitchen aromas are otherworldly – and there is a sense of real auto pilot from Zohra Aunty. She has made this dish many, many times and so has Mursal. It is completely new for me and tremendously exciting. Aunty is careful in showing me quantities, and how to make sure the sauce is the right consistency and that I can taste it as it cooks. We have again this magical moment of being gifted the opportunity to learn from someone, and it's certainly treasured.

Just before eating, we tour the garden with Abdul Uncle: tomatoes, cucumbers, potatoes, mint and a damson tree laden with fruits. We have an impromptu garden picnic with various items being pulled from trees and bushes to taste, with a cameo from their little cat. Uncle tells me how important 'our food' is and that he misses Afghanistan and would like to visit, but he is also resigned to the fact that this probably won't happen. As a family they hold on to their art, literature, poetry and, of course, food. Not only do they hold on to it, but they welcome you to share it with them.

On the one occasion Mursal was able to travel back to Afghanistan, she told me that she tangibly noticed the fact she was a 'diasporic kid', not totally Afghan, and yet not totally British. They couldn't understand her festival bracelets, and her love of silver rather than gold. Culturally this signified that she was less well off, but really silver was a fashion choice rather than a statement of her social standing. After much nattering, we both get excited at all of the possibilities of proactively opting out of the 'hospitality ethnicity trap', which implies that you should only be cooking food from your own culture. I remark on the responses I had being the Head Chef of an Italian restaurant as a Punjabi from Wolverhampton – most of which were praising the food, with only one or two remarking on my 'authenticity'. That's a word that doesn't sit right with me, the more I say it.

Lunch is served with a jar of Afghan chutney – a punchy blend of herbs, garlic, chilli and green tomatoes – some obscenely fluffy rice, salad and some bread. We embark on the various passings and swappings of items to make sure everyone has a little of everything before we sit to eat. It is delicious. Zohra Aunty and Abdul Uncle generously offer more borani banjan and more rice. This brings us on to a moment of friendly competition... Uncle is from Ghorband and Aunty is from Kabul. Now, ask them who's pulao is the best, and we enter into this adorable, respectful tête à tête about which region, and which parent makes the best pulao – different ingredients, different techniques, and both parents making a strong case for each version! We agreed that the only way to find out was to have a cook off to decide, and frankly, I can't wait.

butters

I feel there isn't any need to explain the importance of butter. The enjoyment of butter is something that seems to unite my love for classic French food with my love of Punjabi food. It's the sacred sort of crossover that deep and meaningful friendships are found.

So what did chef Albert Roux and my 90-year-old grandmother have in common? Butter. The love of butter. And here my worlds collide!

Now, this takes a little bit of effort, but really is worth the effort if you're going to make fresh naan, or even baking bread. It lasts well in the fridge and adds a little excitement to everything from a baked potato to your crumpets. Each of these recipes make enough to get you through the week.

green chilli cheese butter

Strong cheese and green chilli is a powerhouse of flavour. Keep an eye on how punchy your chillies are, but use everywhere. I like mine stirred into my scrambled eggs towards the end of cooking, or spread on onion bhaji babka (see page 37).

125g (4½oz) unsalted butter

2 Indian green chillies (or chilli (red pepper) flakes if you don't have fresh chillies)

100g (4½oz) finely grated Cheddar/Parmesan

½ tsp sea salt (kosher salt)

1 Pop all the ingredients into a small food processor and blitz together. Roll into a sausage shape using cling film (plastic wrap) and leave to set in the fridge or pop into a container.

jaggery, date & cashew butter

This butter is the most delicious mix of sweet, crunchy, savoury – it is absolutely joyous spread on hot toast or melted over pancakes.

125g (4½oz) unsalted butter

30g (1oz) jaggery

30g (1oz) fresh dates, pitted

30g (1oz) toasted cashew nuts

½ tsp sea salt (kosher salt)

1 Pop all the ingredients into a small food processor and blitz together. Roll into a sausage shape using cling film (plastic wrap) and leave to set in the fridge or pop into a container.

toasted spice butter

A good time to use up some of your spices from your cupboard, you don't need to be too precious about which spices you have. But I really like the texture and flavour that comes from whole spices.

1 tsp coriander seeds

1 tsp cumin seeds

½ tsp chilli (red pepper) flakes

½ tsp kasoori methi (dried fenugreek)

½ tsp sea salt (kosher salt)

125g (4½oz) unsalted butter, at room temperature

1 Toast the spices, then coarsely crush them and add to the butter. Roll into a sausage shape using cling film (plastic wrap) and leave to set in the fridge or pop into a container.

amchoor onions

Is there anything better than the onions that sizzle under a Desi grill? With some luck, yours have been seasoned with a little amchoor, giving a tangy tartness that cuts the rich fatty meat perfectly. This is a little version of that magic without the need for meat. These are great with anything and give a nice pickley-onion sharpness. Perfect for potato salad too!

MAKES ENOUGH FOR A SMALL JAM JAR

3 tbsp vegetable oil

2 white onions, finely sliced

1 tsp salt

2 tbsp amchoor (dried mango powder)

½ tsp ginger paste

½ tsp nigella seeds (kalonji)

1 Heat the oil in a frying pan (skillet) over a medium–high heat and add the onions. You can sauté them over a fairly high heat – caramelization will only add flavour here, so don't be shy. After about 10 minutes, season with the salt, amchoor, ginger and nigella seeds and fry for a minute longer. Remove from the heat and this is ready to use, or you can allow it to cool and keep in the fridge for a couple of days.

jeera roasties

I don't know of anyone who doesn't love roast potatoes. These came about as a little addition to a rather splendid spin on Sunday lunch, something to sit well with a whole roast chicken, or indeed the pork belly in this book (see page 130). They work with everything really, and since most of us usually have a little turmeric and cumin in the cupboard this is a nice way to give your crunchy roasties a touch more glamour. I add a little semolina because it amplifies the crunch and I love the texture.

SERVES | 4

1kg (2lb 4oz) floury (starchy) potatoes

1 tsp fine salt

2 heaped tbsp fine semolina (farina)

2 tsp sea salt

1 tsp ground turmeric

2 tsp cumin seeds

8 tbsp vegetable oil

1 Peel your potatoes and cut the small ones in half and any that are really big into 4–5 pieces. Put them into a pan of cold water, with the salt. Bring to the boil and cook for 10 minutes from boiling.

2 Preheat the oven to 180°C fan/200°C/400°F/gas mark 6 and pop in a large roasting tray to warm.

3 Check the potatoes are done by gently inserting a knife into the chunks: if it slides off easily, the potatoes are cooked. Drain them well in a colander (strainer) and allow them to steam and dry out a little. Sprinkle them with the semolina, salt, turmeric and cumin seeds and gently coat. Take the roasting tray from the oven, carefully spoon over the oil, then lay out the potatoes nicely so they have a little space. Pop them straight back into the oven for about 35 minutes, making sure you turn them as they crisp. Serve immediately.

spicy crushed potatoes

A little bowl full of potato joy! Potatoes are such an amazing vehicle for flavour. You can spice up, spice down, add peas and a little Cheddar if you fancy. You can form this mixture into little aloo tikkis that can be baked or pan-fried – totally delicious and marvellously easy. The trick is to cut your potato into even sizes to ensure consistent cooking and to avoid lumps. You can opt for a plant-based version of this by omitting the butter.

SERVES | 4

1kg (2lb 4oz) waxy potatoes, peeled and cut into even-sized pieces

1 tbsp veg oil

30g (1oz) butter, optional

2 spring onions, (scallions), finely sliced

½ tsp fine salt

TEMPERED SPICE

2 tbsp vegetable oil

½ tsp cumin seeds

½ tsp black mustard seeds

8 small fresh curry leaves

¼ tsp ground turmeric

Pinch of sea salt

½ tsp garlic paste

½ tsp green chilli paste

1 Put your potatoes into cold salted water, bring to the boil and cook for 15 minutes or so. You can tell they are done if you insert a knife into the pieces and they slide off easily. Drain the potatoes in a colander (strainer) and pop the colander back on top of the cooking pan off the heat to steam for a little while.

2 Pop the potatoes into the dry cooking pan and gently press with the back of a spoon to the desired texture.

3 Pop the oil in another pan and warm gently. Add all the tempered spice ingredients and heat until the mustard seeds sizzle and pop, then turn the mix into your potatoes. Serve immediately, topped with finely sliced spring onions.

spicy mango salad with whole herbs & mooli

This is such a vibrant salad: big on flavour and freshness. If you want to add shredded leftover chicken or Chettinad duck (see page 161) it's equally delicious. You can add a little fresh chilli if you like but I really love the fresh sweetness of the mango and the refreshing crunch of the mooli (daikon). It is such a wonderful dish to make as a platter. You don't need to follow the rules here too much; I would suggest it's wise to invest in a julienne peeler because it reduces faff and can make your salads look as if you've taken an age to cut delicate little strands of vegetables when in reality you haven't. It's not cheating … it's clever! Equally, though, you can cut the ingredients in a more rustic chunky way – or a fine dice.

SERVES | 4

Juice of 1 lime

1 tsp chaat masala

1 tsp grated (shredded) ginger

1 small mooli (daikon)

1 medium carrot

1 red onion

2 ripe but firm mangos

1 small bunch of mint

1 small bunch of coriander (cilantro)

¼ tsp sea salt

10 small red breakfast radishes, thinly sliced

Small handful of toasted peanuts

1 Juice the lime straight into a large mixing bowl, add the chaat masala and ginger and mix well. Use your julienne peeler to shred your mooli and carrot. Slice your red onion finely and add everything to the bowl.

2 If you are using a green mango, wash it well and use a regular peeler to take off some of the tough skin. Then use your julienne peeler to cut the flesh off into ribbons. If you have a sweet mango, take off the cheeks and sides, remove the skin and slice or dice the flesh into the bowl.

3 Pick your mint leaves off the tough stalks and add them to the salad – use the stalks for tea if you like. Do the same with the coriander – putting all of the leaves into the salad. Then chop the stalks as finely as you can before adding these too. Finish with the salt, radishes and toasted peanuts.

masala dukkah

I really am mad for texture in my food – and it's so easy to amp up a simple salad, breads or dips with a little extra level of flavour and crunch. This is my version of an Indian-style dukkah. If you prefer a certain nut you are welcome to use that and, if you have an allergy, just opt for some delicious mixed seeds. The key is not to over-blitz everything so you can enjoy the flavour of each individual spice.

1 tsp coriander seeds

1 tsp cumin seeds

1 tsp fennel seeds

1 tsp sea salt (kosher salt)

½ tsp nigella seeds (kalonjii)

½ tsp chilli (red pepper) flakes

½ ajwain (carom) seeds

3 tbsp cashew nuts

3 tbsp pumpkin seeds

1 tsp white sesame seeds

1 tbsp rapeseed (canola) oil

1 Pop everything into a non-stick frying pan (skillet) and toast gently for 15 minutes over a medium heat, making sure that the nuts and seeds don't burn. I prefer to do this in a pan because the aroma of everything toasting is utterly delicious. If you want to pop it onto a baking tray and into a low oven, don't use the fan setting, otherwise you will see everything flying around your oven.

2 When it has all toasted nicely, and you see some golden colour on your nuts and smell the aroma of the spices, remove them from the heat and blitz in a chopper for a couple of moments. Keep the mix fairly coarse and allow to cool completely before storing in an airtight container.

3 If you feel like seasoning up or adding more spice – now is the time.

EATING

Sprinkle into salads, on soups, roasted potatoes, vegetables or with breads that have been dipped into oil.

Throw over avocado toast or scrambled eggs too.

tempered spice slaw

This salad is about as easy as it gets. You can do the prep up to two days before you need it and it tastes amazing two days later – I mean, what else is needed? I don't like heavy, mayonnaise-laden slaws but I do love the crunch of fresh veggies simply dressed with citrus. Again, consider this a foundation of ingredients to play with. You can add cold blanched rice noodles or tofu. Cooked prawns (shrimp), chicken or any leftover proteins will create something a little more substantial. My personal preference is to make it when I do the slow-cooked pork belly (see page 161) so the following day you can have leftover roast pork and slaw sandwiches with a lick of achaari mayo.

SERVES | 2–4

1 sweetheart (hispi) or small white cabbage (or ¼ of a large one, ½ if you have guests)

2 good-sized carrots

1 small bunch of spring onions (scallions), trimmed

1 small red onion

2 (bell) peppers (red and yellow are great), trimmed and deseeded

1 long red chilli, trimmed, deseeded and finely chopped

1 small thumb of fresh ginger, sliced as finely as you or grated (shredded)

3 tbsp white vinegar

Juice of 2 limes

3 tbsp vegetable oil

½ tsp cumin seeds

½ tsp black mustard seeds

½ tsp fennel seeds

½ tsp nigella seeds (kalonji)

Pinch of salt

½ bunch of coriander (cilantro), chopped

1 You can use a mandolin, julienne peeler or chop by hand for this. Ideally you want the veg to be nice and fine.

2 Quarter your cabbage to make it easier to manage. Then shred it as finely as you can. Tip into a large bowl or dish. Peel your carrots, then either coarsely grate (shred) them on a box grater or use a julienne peeler to create some lovely strips. Finely slice your spring onions, red onion and peppers and add to the cabbage and carrot mix, along with the chilli and ginger. Pour in the vinegar and lime juice and mix well.

3 Warm the oil in a small saucepan or frying pan (skillet), add the cumin, mustard, fennel and nigella seeds and let them sizzle. When they begin to pop, pour the hot oil mix over the slaw, season with the salt and finish with some chopped coriander. Mix well and serve.

Sweets

" Desserts to me always feel like a treat – and it isn't just the eating of them, it's the making I love.

In my childhood, sugar came in all forms, from penny sweets and chocolate to jalebis and besan, mithai, ras gulas, biscuits, gulaab jammun and rasmalai. There was always room for meethi cheez – a litle something sweet.

One of the easier parts of British cuisine that our early generations could acclimatise to was puddings: trifles, sponges, custard, cakes, fresh cream, jam tarts, roly polys – a new world of desserts had been discovered, and for my family, embraced warmly. I remember my father telling me how he couldn't believe his luck when he encountered his first school dinner, after polishing off a meal that had mash and gravy (probably a pie), out came a jam sponge and custard. To his amazement, this happened not just once a week, but every day at school.

I have always been into biscuits, and I wonder if this again is one of those cultural hereditary marvels that I have inherited. I would like to see some data on how many biscuits the South Asian community purchase annually because I'm quite sure we have collectively upheld the share price of McVities.

Our cupboards were full of the good stuff that the 90s English food scene offered: Bird's Custard, Angel Delight, jelly, Viennetta, steamed sponges, Cadbury's chocolate, tins of rice pudding and almost every 'biskut' known to man. A few dishes that always featured for us were apple pie, sponges and custard, pancakes with ice cream and of course Mrs Gidda's Trifle, the recipe to which I am thrilled to share with you in this chapter.

The classic Punjabi sweet treats soon became too sweet for me. My Biji had diabetes and so does my father, so our dessert consumption was drastically reduced – and more than this, so was our taste for sugar. We made custards and cakes with 75% less sugar and became quite accustomed to it. My father Hardeep says that you can reduce the

sugar in almost anything by a third before you can identify a noticeable difference in flavour. However, it is not just flavour that the sugar supports, it is texture and finish, so it is best to manage your expectations with the adjustment of sugar.

Desserts to me always feel like a treat – and it isn't just the eating of them, it's the making I love. Pastry and desserts often require a type of scientific discipline, which 98% of the time I lack completely. I have to try very hard indeed to supress my inner freewheeling culinary pirate. The temptation to add this and that is often how the next dish is conceived, but not always with immediate success.

I wanted to find a way to bring some of the more classic desserts I grew up eating into a collection of playful, modern recipes for you to enjoy. It is a wonderful opportunity to use some of the spices you have in your store cupboard to create something fun and a little bit different.

Mrs Gidda's trifle

Sukey Gidda is the Queen of My World. And here we have perhaps her most iconic dish: trifle. Now of course you are welcome, most welcome, to make your own sponge, make homemade jelly, custard from scratch. But, frankly, my mother believed the best part of trifle-making was the eating and, in turn I feel exactly the same. She always had a giggle when it came to soaking the sponges – usually because of the very generous free-pour of Malibu, followed closely by 'and one for luck'. This is about enjoyment, nostalgia, love and celebration – and I will always make this for my family to celebrate her in all of her glory.

SERVES | 4–6

1 x box trifle sponges or sponge fingers (ladyfingers)

250g (9oz) strawberries, hulled, large ones quartered or halved

200g (7oz) fresh pineapple, diced

200g (7oz) raspberries

200g (7oz) ripe mango, diced

Generous glug of Malibu rum, say 180–200ml (about ¾ cup)

2 sachets or 70g (2½oz) quick-set jelly (jello)

105g (3½oz) Bird's custard powder

850ml (scant 3¾ cups) milk

250ml (1 cup) whipping (heavy) cream

1 tsp icing (confectioners') sugar

Splash of vanilla extract

Handful of toasted almond shards

1 Find yourself a good-sized (20cm/8in) bowl, trifle dish or just use anything you have that will fit everything in!

2 Line the bottom and sides with your trifle sponges. Tip in all the fruit and spread over the sponges.

3 Pour a glug of Malibu over the fruit and sponges. Leave it to soak in while you make the jelly (jello) following the pack instructions and allow to cool slightly.

4 Pour the jelly over the fruit and sponges and put in the fridge to set.

5 Your custard prep can be done in a jug in a microwave or you can do it in a pan. Mix the custard powder with a splash of milk and stir until there are no lumps. Add the remaining milk and bring to the boil, stirring constantly, to avoid any lumps. Cook out for 10 minutes until thick. I don't add sugar as everything else adds more than enough sugar for me but add a teaspoon if you want.

6 Allow the custard to cool for a few minutes before pouring over your jelly evenly. You should have clear layers now.

7 Allow to cool at room temperature before returning it to the fridge to set.

8 Whip the cream with the icing sugar and vanilla until firm ribbons appear. Top the custard with the whipped cream and sprinkle over the toasted almonds.

gulab jammun semifreddo

We made a serious amount of semifreddo during my time at Bernardi's restaurant. White espresso, peach, chocolate, gianduja … you name it, we made it. While we did make our own ice cream too, I really have always loved the no-churn element of semifreddo – it's almost the Italian equivalent of kulfi. This version celebrates one particular golden globe of joy that is loved by all South Asians: gulab jammun. Now of course you can make everything from scratch – but personally I like to pop to a sweet centre (store) and just buy them.

SERVES | 6–8

3 free-range egg whites

80g (2¾oz) sugar

½ tsp ground cardamom

Tiny pinch of saffron powder

240ml (scant 1 cup) double (heavy) cream, cold

5 gulab jamun, broken down into pieces

1 Whisk your egg whites in a large clean bowl until they turn white and start to firm up. When they do so, add half the sugar and whisk to stiff glossy peaks before adding the cardamom and saffron powder.

2 In another bowl, whip your cream until you begin to see ribbons. Then add the remaining sugar and whip until soft peaks appear. You don't want to overwhip, but it isn't catastrophic if you do, although the texture may be a little grainy.

3 Carefully fold a quarter of the cream into the meringue, trying not to knock out all of the air. Repeat this process until you have used all the cream. Then gently fold in the gulab jammun.

4 Line a plastic container or loaf tin (pan) with greaseproof (parchment) paper and pour the mixture in and freeze for at least 3 hours. I like to use a loaf tin – so I can sandwich the semifreddo with some old-school wafers.

Mamiji's kheer

Kheer is a rich rice pudding, often containing nuts, cardamom, sometimes saffron or maybe raisins. It is a dessert my mum never really made – because 'Gulshan always made it so perfectly' – so here it is, Mamiji's kheer. I can tell you, having eaten many, many, many bowls, it is as delicious cold as is it freshly made. You can use plant-based milk for this – almond milk works nicely – but you do need to stir it to make sure it doesn't catch on the pan. Needless to say, you can also make it with semi-skimmed dairy milk, but I don't suggest skimmed – this dish is a whole-milk, fat-rich dish, so just enjoy it!

SERVES | 4

70g (2½oz) basmati rice

1 tsp ghee or butter

3–4 green cardamom pods, crushed

1.4 litres (6 cups) whole milk

2 tbsp soft brown or golden caster (superfine) sugar

50g chopped nuts (any – I like pistachios and almonds)

Raisins or currants, optional

1 Rinse the rice until the water runs clear. Then soak the rice in enough water for 20–30 minutes. Drain the rice through a colander or strainer and set aside.

2 Heat a heavy-bottomed pan over a medium heat. Add the ghee and then the drained rice and the cardamom pods.

3 Toss the rice with the ghee and cardamom for 1–2 minutes, stirring constantly, until aromatic.

4 Pour the milk into the pan and stir well. Increase the heat to medium–high and allow the milk to come to the boil, this will take about 10–12 minutes. Stir occasionally so that the milk doesn't catch on the base of the pan.

5 Once the milk has come to the boil, let the kheer cook for about 25 minutes over a low heat, stirring every couple of minutes. The milk will reduce considerably after 25 minutes, the kheer will look thick and the rice will be cooked. If you want super-thick kheer, cook for a further 15 minutes at this point.

6 Stir in the sugar and nuts. Cook the kheer for 5 minutes longer to dissolve the sugar completely. Don't worry if your kheer doesn't look very thick at this point – it will continue to thicken as it cools down.

7 Garnish with nuts and raisins, if using.

Johnnie Walker crème caramel

Johnnie Walker whisky always reminds me of my grandfather. It was his favourite whisky – and I do love the warmth it gives the caramel in this classic French pudding. Naturally you can make it without, but this is a little tribute to a truly great man, my Babaji. This makes six if you use individual 150ml (½ cup) ramekins or foil moulds, but equally you can make a large one in a dish you are able to turn out after cooking in a bain-marie.

SERVES | 4–6

CUSTARD

50g (1¾oz) caster (superfine) sugar

3 large free-range eggs and 2 yolks

500ml (2 cups) whole milk

1 vanilla pod

CARAMEL

160g (5¾oz) soft brown sugar

4 tbsp water

3 tbsp Johnnie Walker whisky (or bourbon)

1 Preheat the oven to 170°C fan/190°C/375°F/gas mark 5. To make the caramel, put the sugar, water and whisky in a pan. Place over a medium–low heat and allow the sugar to dissolve. Don't stir it, just carefully swirl the pan when you can see the sugar has melted and is starting to colour. You need to keep an eye on this to make sure it doesn't go too far, but you want a nice golden hue and even consistency. Divide the caramel between your moulds.

2 Whisk the sugar, eggs and yolks until the mixture is pale, smooth and light.

3 Pour the milk into a second pan, split the vanilla pod lengthways, scrape out the seeds and add both seeds and pod to the milk. Allow the milk to come to the boil, but don't let it boil. Remove the vanilla pod from the pan.

4 Carefully and slowly pour the hot milk over the eggs, mixing well and stirring vigorously to make sure no lumps form.

5 Pass this mix through a sieve (strainer) into a jug. A regular sieve should allow all of the vanilla seeds to pass through.

6 Divide the custard between the moulds. Put the moulds in a roasting dish, and pour enough boiling water into the dish so that it reaches just over halfway up the sides. Bake for about 18–20 minutes until the tops feel set but still have a wobble like panna cotta. Remove them from their bain-marie and allow them to cool. Ideally you need to refrigerate for at least 5 hours or overnight.

7 When you are ready to serve, gently use your thumb to tease the custards from the sides of the moulds; this should be fairly easy. Pop a serving plate on top of each mould, then quickly invert both mould and plate so the caramel pops out onto the plate. If you struggle, you can dip the moulds into warm water for a few seconds to help them release.

gajar halwa carrot cake

Gajar halwa is an amazing dish made from cooking down carrots in milk with some sugar and a little cardamom. There are many, many different versions, some use condensed milk, nuts, khoya (a type of unsweetened milk solid) and many families have their own special little additions. I wasn't crazy about it as a child but, as I have grown up, making it with a bit less sugar has really made me enjoy the flavour much more. In this instance I have worked it into a super-moist spiced carrot cake – a format that is pleasing to almost everyone! You can create a large round cake but I like to use a brownie pan and cut it into squares.

SERVES | 6 GENEROUSLY

65ml (generous ¼ cup) vegetable oil

60g (2¼oz) muscovado (soft dark brown) sugar

50g (1¾oz) caster (superfine) sugar

120g (4¼oz) plain (all-purpose) flour

½ tsp baking powder

½ tsp bicarbonate of soda (baking soda)

1 tsp ground cinnamon

1 tsp ground black cardamom

1 tsp ground green cardamom

¼ tsp ground cloves

200g (7oz) carrots, well washed, peeled and coarsely grated (shredded) on the largest side of a grater

1 free-range egg, whisked

40g (1½oz) natural (plain) yoghurt

FROSTING

400g (14oz) full-fat cream cheese

½ can condensed milk

Zest of 1 orange

Toasted pistachios

1 Preheat the oven to 170°C fan/190°C/375°F/gas mark 5. Line a brownie pan or cake tin (cake pan) with baking paper.

2 Put the oil and sugars into your mixer and combine well until pale and fluffy. Add all the dry ingredients and mix on a low speed – then add the oil and yoghurt.

3 Scrape down the bowl and make sure everything is mixed well.

4 Pour into your lined cake tin and bake for 45 minutes. Insert a skewer to check the cake is cooked – cook for another 5–10 minutes if needed.

5 Remove from the tin and allow to cool on a wire rack.

6 Meanwhile, lightly beat the cream cheese and condensed milk, adding most of the orange zest. Pop this in the fridge to firm up before spreading.

7 Once your cake is cooled, spread the frosting over the top, sprinkle with pistachios and remaining orange zest and enjoy.

cardamom & pistachio gelato

If we speak of magical flavour combinations, cardamom and pistachio have got to be up there with the best. Effectively this is a riff on kulfi, except it has a much softer texture when made in an ice-cream machine. If you don't have a machine, you can simply freeze it in a container to make a bar and cut slices much like the gulab jammun semifreddo on page 199.

SERVES | 4

2 free-range egg yolks

55g (2oz) caster (superfine) sugar

250ml (1 cup) milk

100ml (scant ½ cup) condensed milk

75ml (scant ⅓ cup) double (heavy) cream

65g (2¼oz) pistachio paste (the good stuff)

2 tsp ground cardamom

Handful of toasted pistachios, chopped

1 Beat the egg yolks and sugar together in a large bowl until fluffy and light.

2 Put the milk, condensed milk and cream in a pan and bring to the boil. Gently add to the eggs, stirring continuously, before mixing in the pistachio paste and cardamom. Return it to the pan over the heat and use a sugar thermometer to indicate when the temperature reaches 82°C (179°F). Remove from the heat.

3 At this point, chill the gelato before churning in an ice-cream machine. If you aren't churning, pour into a loaf tin (pan) lined with two layers of cling film (plastic wrap) so that you can take it out to slice it, or pop it into a plastic container that will fit in your freezer. Before freezing, sprinkle with the toasted pistachios.

chai spiced shortbread

I have never met a Punjabi who didn't love shortbread. Elaborate gifted boxes of Marks & Spencer's finest commemorative tins, ones with Scotty dogs, images of London, tartan – you name it, we had it and we loved it. My grandparents were particularly fond of it – and when we would visit India we would take with us plenty of biscuits to keep their stash topped up. This is a classic shortbread recipe with a little sprinkle of some of those amazing spices you find in masala chai – just for a little bit of magic.

SERVES | 4 GREEDILY

250g (9oz) soft butter

70g (2½oz) golden caster (superfine) sugar

250g (9oz) plain (all-purpose) flour

60g (2¼oz) cornflour (cornstarch)

Pinch of fine salt

CHAI SPICE

¾ tsp ground cinnamon

½ teaspoon ground green cardamom

¼ tsp ground black cardamom

½ tsp ground ginger

½ tsp ground cloves

1 Preheat the oven to 170°C fan/190°C/375°F/gas mark 5.

2 Whisk together the butter and sugar until well combined and fluffy.

3 Sift in the flour, cornflour, salt and chai spice and mix gently, you don't want to go crazy here as overworking the dough isn't good.

4 Mix until combined and then press into a baking tray lined with greaseproof (parchment) paper. You can use a sandwich cake tin (pan) if you like. Now you can use a fork to make the little holes synonymous with shortbread and gently mark out the wedges or finger shapes you will cut later.

5 Bake for about 1 hour. Then remove from the oven and cut through your markings while still a little warm. Allow to cool and enjoy with a cup of masala chai.

almond & brown butter madeleines

Madeleines are such a joy to eat. To get the classic shape, you do need to purchase a madeleine tray but it isn't essential: cupcake trays, with or without cases, also work nicely. My preference is to eat these warm from the oven, with a few cups of fresh masala chai. Equally they can accompany your pistachio gelato or some ready-made ice cream for a speedy dessert.

MAKES | 12

200g (7oz) unsalted butter

2 large free-range eggs

90g (3¼oz) caster (superfine) sugar

80g (2¾oz) self-raising (self-rising) flour

30g (1oz) ground almonds

¼ tsp ground cardamom

2 tbsp whole milk

1 Preheat the oven to 190°C fan/210°C/400°F/gas mark 6. Put your butter into a small pan and melt over a medium heat until the butter begins to sizzle and foam. Keep an eye on it and gently tilt the pan to ensure everything is browning nicely. When you can smell the butter toasting and it is turning brown, remove it from the heat and set it to one side. When it has cooled slightly, stir the butter so that the milk solids mix throughout and pour into a measuring jug or cup so you have 100ml (scant ½ cup) of liquid butter. Use any remaining butter to lightly grease the madeleine tray.

2 Whisk together the eggs and sugar until doubled in volume and pale and fluffy. Sift in the flour and mix well.

3 Add the ground almonds, cardamom and milk and pour in the cooled butter. Mix well and leave the batter to rest for 15 minutes.

4 You can use a piping bag if you have one to pipe the batter into the madeleine tray, otherwise just spoon it into the moulds evenly.

5 Bake for 10 minutes until golden.

black cardamom custard tart

For my last *Great British Menu* dessert – I did a tribute dessert to Alfred Bird, who created Bird's custard powder for his wife who had an egg allergy. It was a joy to create because Bird's custard has always been, and still is, a store-cupboard favourite. I grew up eating it with all the delicious sponges and trifles I was lucky enough to eat at home – and I am sure I don't need to explain to anyone that making crème anglaise or crème pâtissière wasn't really a thing in nineties Wolverhampton! I have always loved custard – and I always will. In this version I have tweaked the recipe to incorporate black cardamom and nutmeg for spicing. Remarkably the pastry also contains custard powder, making it an entirely eggless custard tart!

SERVES | 8–10

PASTRY

350g (12oz) plain (all-purpose) flour

2 tbsp Bird's custard powder

170g (6oz) chilled butter

70g (scant ⅓ cup) water

A pinch of salt

170g (6oz) icing (confectioners') sugar

FILLING

6 tbsp Bird's custard powder – not too heaped!

500ml (2 cups) whole milk

500ml (2 cups) double (heavy) cream

2 tbsp caster (superfine) sugar

½ tsp ground green cardamom

½ tsp ground black cardamom

A good grinding of nutmeg

1 Preheat the oven to 180°C fan/200°C/400°F/gas mark 6. To make your sweet pastry, mix all the pastry ingredients together to create a smooth, even dough. Roll into a ball and chill in the fridge for 15 minutes.

2 Roll out the pastry to a 5mm (¼in) thickness, place in a 22cm (9in) tart tin (pan), line with greaseproof (parchment) paper and add some baking beans. Blind bake for 12–15 minutes until golden. Set aside to cool.

3 Meanwhile, make the filling. Whisk the custard powder with a glug of the milk and make sure there are no lumps. Put the cream, remaining milk and the sugar in a small pan and bring to boil, then add the custard mix, stirring constantly until it thickens. Add the ground green and black cardamom and nutmeg, mixing thoroughly.

4 Pour directly into your tart case and finish with a liberal grating of nutmeg. Chill the tart before serving.

Chai & Spice
Nisha Kudhail

I just want to take a moment to say that the first thing I noticed on arriving at Nisha's home, was the smell of masala chai bubbling on the stove. Joy was imminent – and we hadn't even got to the barfi yet! Nisha told me stories of big family get-togethers when she was a child, usually inclusive of many extended family members, grandparents on both sides of her family and, of course, many aunts, uncles and cousins. As you can imagine, it was all about coming together to celebrate over food, drink and as she says 'endless cups of cha'. The kitchen would be where the grandmothers, mothers and aunts would get together to cook up a homemade feast, with each woman having her own speciality and strength in the kitchen. She was totally in awe of them as they cooked and mesmerized by their talent and skill. Ladoos would be rolled, exacting free-pours of sugar for the perfect gulab jammun or jalebi syrups and a production line of mattis (savoury biscuits, perfect with tea) would be occurring almost simultaneously through the kitchen.

As a child she wasn't really crazy about the tidying up after all those delicious meals, so she found herself gravitating to the kitchens where all of the magic was happening. This resonates with me too, although initially I was always in the kitchen because it allowed me to get my little hands on something delicious well before it started making its merry way to the table and our guests. Nisha began running supper clubs to cook delicious home-cooked Desi food for people in their homes – but quickly realized it was the mithai (sweet treats) that she loved making the most.

It was Nisha's uncle, a chef in Southall, who she called to ask about barfi-making on a larger scale. Naturally he was adept at making all manner of delicious traditional dishes, including samosas and various barfis, and was only too happy to spend a little time in the kitchen to show Nisha how to make these delicious classics. Her aunts and grandmothers provided yet more knowledge on technique and flavourings. Unsurprisingly she was hooked, and having mastered the technique it was really important to make her offering personal. Her husband has a nut allergy and for Nisha this meant that a large selection of mithai was totally out of bounds for him, leaving him (and many others) with a really restricted selection of items and flavours. I love how she tells me, 'I created it so he could enjoy it too', which I really can't see as anything other than a profound act of love. She giveth barfi!

So she set to work tweaking classic recipes to reflect a new palate, one that required a little less sugar and a lot less nuts, but also one that mindfully positioned her product not just as barfi (to those of us in the know), but as 'Indian fudge'. She chose to steer away from the super-sweet mithai of her childhood and create inventive and exciting flavours that could become new favourites. She began making barfi for friends and family, to mark various religious festivals and for family get-togethers before launching her business, Chai & Spice. Her style is North Indian which uses a mix of milk powder, cream, condensed milk and spices as a starting point for every flavour she creates, and then she looks at what flavours would be exciting.

I make things that I want to eat!

Her business was initially created for British Asians who love gifting traditional sweets but want more modern and inventive flavours. Some are looking for something nostalgic, some love to experiment, but other people adore fudge and Indian food and want to discover something new. I love that she has found a way to open the door for people to try her product by giving them the opportunity to become familiar with it. There must be many people who have walked past our wonderful South Asian sweet centres and shops and glanced in at row after row of abundant treats, but perhaps don't have the courage to walk in and ask about them, let alone try them. And so the door remains closed for them. They will never know the magical taste of milk cake, khoya barfi, besan ladoo and rasgulla. I find this tremendously sad. Surely we should all be going in to any shop with something delicious on display, and celebrating both the culture and the people who are making it. There is too much deliciousness to eat and no time to waste with shyness or fear of the unknown. We should explore!

Watching Nisha work is joyous. She has military discipline that is matched by a completely intrinsic, holistic understanding of ingredients and their outcomes. She has used playful ingredients like Biscoff or Oreo that keep the younger generation excited and interested by new flavours in such classic mithai, which frankly is very clever. Her gorgeous three children are on hand as taste testers for her new creations and love to give their feedback. I am both jealous and thrilled by this, because this is where excitement about cooking and

My style is North Indian, which uses a mix of milk powder, cream, condensed milk and spices as a starting point for every flavour I create.

eating begins at a young age – when you are included and involved. Sometimes, this is why we become chefs.

Growing up in Southall, Nisha was surrounded by that glorious infrastructure of multicultural retail. She looked forward to the seasonal fruits that would become available, including lychees, cane sugar and, of course, mangoes in the summer, and winter was a time for baked apples, sprinkled with spices and topped with crumble. These are the moments that have helped her create new flavours, constantly keeping interest and also acknowledging wider religious celebrations and holidays. She passes me some lemon and poppyseed to try and it really is unlike any kind of barfi I have tried, totally unique and really delicious. Autumn is the start of apple crumble flavour and at Christmas there is mince pie barfi. I think it's equal measures of creating new exciting flavours for people to try and keeping her creative energy in the kitchen – something I really appreciate.

As we start work on her signature lychee and rose barfi, she tells me how she really always wanted to cook a traditional sweet, but using all natural ingredients with no artificial food colourings. So it could have less sugar, nothing artificial and be nut-free and still be utterly delicious. She uses condensed milk but no additional sugar and is uncompromising with the quality of her ingredients. We make the barfi with fresh lychee juice and lots of it, a favourite of Nisha's from childhood – this was one of the first flavours she created. The texture is very similar to a traditional barfi but has a really incredible floral note from both the lychee and the rose petals and when I am lucky enough to try it, I can't help but notice what a difference using less sugar and replacing it with lychee juice has made. After lychee and rose came vanilla chai barfi. They are really special.

One of her earliest and most beautiful memories is the traditional Indian welcome of

tea and endless snacks, with every greeting and goodbye always followed by 'Cha da cup peelo' which simply translates to 'Have a cup of tea'. It is this hospitality, known and noted across the world that inspired Chai & Spice. The creation of bite-sized and moreish treats to enjoy with a cup of hot masala tea represents her British Indian upbringing. At this point as we chat, there is a small moment where it feels like we may in fact be related. After some note swapping, it turns out we're not, although this is another moment in the journey of writing this book where I see we are 'relating', celebrating and sharing the same heart-warming traditions that so many of us share. Even as Nisha speaks with me I can see generation after generation in homes from all backgrounds having that special 'cha da cup' moment, and I sincerely hope it lasts forever.

As we drink tea and eat barfi, she tells me about how within her business she is able to celebrate many different festivals and religious celebrations and offer something special to everyone. Along with Diwali, the celebrations of Rakhri, Christmas, Nowruz and Eid are also proving popular with people wanting to send something special to their loved ones. By hand Nisha fills dates with her barfi mix, before boxing them and sending them out for Eid. Now, if anyone has pitted a date and stuffed it, you will know how tricky this can be, but multiply that by a few hundred, before boxing (also done by hand), and you'll understand the importance of craft and loving what you do.

Nisha is a perfectionist and my time in the kitchen with her was full of the most amazing shared experience and humour at various Punjabi cultural nuances, all while she shares her passion for not just doing what she does, but doing it to be the very best it possibly can. I love this about her. She has made her business to celebrate a facet of her culture and has welcomed everyone to enjoy. When she tells me she is proud of what she has created, I cannot help but feel that pride too.

fennel & cashew biscotti

My time at Bernardi's restaurant was full of the finest Italian produce – and we loved creating playful takes on classic recipes. Biscotti are twice-baked biscuits perfect for dunking in chai, or serving with desserts and coffee. This recipe combines delicious cashews with fennel – and it really is a delight. If you don't like cashews you can use almonds or hazelnuts instead. Once the biscotti are made they last for a good few weeks in an airtight jar – or at least I would assume they do; mine tend to get eaten fairly quickly.

MAKES | 20

350g (12oz) plain (all-purpose) flour

2 tsp baking powder

220g (7¾oz) golden caster (superfine) sugar

2 tsp fennel seeds

120g (4¼oz) cashew nuts, roughly broken in half

1 tsp ground ginger

Zest of 1 unwaxed lemon

3 free-range eggs, whisked

2 tbsp fine semolina (farina), for dusting

1 Preheat the oven to 165°C fan/185°C/360°F/gas mark 4½. Line one or two baking trays with baking paper.

2 Pop all the dry ingredients (apart from the semolina) into a large mixing bowl and then add the whisked eggs. Use a fork to bring the dough together.

3 Dust your work surface with the fine semolina, then turn out the dough. Divide into 4 balls and roll these into sausage shapes.

4 Carefully place on the lined baking trays, allowing plenty of space for expansion on the tray, so don't put the rolls too close together. Bake for about 25 minutes or until the dough has started to colour and is holding firm.

5 I would give these rolls about 5 minutes to rest so you can then handle them. If they are too hot they are difficult to slice and, if they are too cold, your slices may just crumble.

6 Transfer the rolls to a board. You will need to cut them into 1cm (½in) slices, then put these slices back on the baking trays. Bake for 10 minutes on each side until they are crunchy and golden.

ginger & jaggery pudding

This is, to all intents and purposes, a supercharged sticky toffee pudding – something betwixt the classic British pud and the sticky Jamaican ginger cake. I have used jaggery as I really enjoy the richness and depth of flavour that it brings. Serve with ice cream or Bird's custard.

SERVES | 9

SPONGE

175g (6oz) pitted Medjool dates, roughly chopped

1 teabag (I use cardamom or masala chai)

1 tsp bicarbonate of soda (baking soda)

175g (6oz) soft salted butter

60g (2oz) jaggery powder

20g (¾oz) golden caster (superfine) sugar

2 free-range eggs

100ml (scant ½ cup) whole milk

1 tsp vanilla extract

3 tsp ground ginger

175g (6oz) self-raising (self-rising) flour

CARAMEL

150ml (scant ⅔ cup) double (heavy) cream

80g (2¾oz) jaggery powder

75g (2½oz) lightly salted butter

1 tsp ground ginger

Pinch of salt

1 Preheat the oven to 180°C fan/200°C/400°F/gas mark 6. Pour 150ml (scant ⅔ cup) of just-boiled water over the dates and add the teabag. Add the bicarbonate of soda, mix well and allow to steep for 15 minutes before removing the teabag. Blend the date mix until smooth.

2 Meanwhile, cream together the butter and jaggery powder until smooth and fluffy. Add the eggs, milk, vanilla and ground ginger. Then add the date mixture.

3 Sift in the flour and mix well.

4 Pour into an 18cm (7in) square baking dish or a lined cake tin (pan) and bake for 35–40 minutes or until a skewer comes out clean. Remove from the oven and rest.

5 Put all the ingredients for the caramel in a saucepan and bring to the boil, stirring. When the mix is smooth and golden, pour over the cake.

kada prashad clafoutis

If you have never had kada prashad it is going to be very difficult for me to explain the magic of this flavour. Prashad is offered as a sweet blessing in Gudwaras to all those who visit as a gift of sustenance and blessings – you never decline when it is offered to you. It is made with sugar, water, ghee and wholewheat flour. The remarkably distinct flavour comes from browning the flour in ghee or butter, which creates a wonderful golden hue and an amazing noisette nuttiness – enhanced by the sugar. Texturally this reminds me a lot of clafoutis – so I have recreated a version that toasts the almonds and flour in the same way. You can select any fruits you like for this – but I have used blackberries as I really like the contrast between sharp fruit and nutty pudding.

SERVES | 4

40g (1½oz) butter

30g (1oz) wholemeal (wholewheat) flour

50g (1¾oz) ground almonds

2 eggs and 2 yolks

250ml (1 cup) double (heavy) cream

100g (3½oz) caster (superfine) sugar

1 punnet of blackberries

Pouring cream, to serve

1 Preheat the oven to 190°C fan/210°C/400°F/gas mark 6. In a saucepan, heat your butter until it turns golden and nutty. Don't be scared, it should go a deep brown. Cool slightly.

2 Put the eggs, yolks, cream and sugar into a jug and blend until smooth. Add the browned butter, flour and almonds, blend again and pour into an 18cm (7in) oven dish. Scatter in the blackberries and bake for 25 minutes.

3 Allow to rest for 5 minutes before serving with pouring cream.

mango & lime posset

A posset is a very easy-to-make dessert and the contrast between tart limes and sweet mango is a perfect treat to finish of a meal. I made a posset for the semi-final of The Roux Scholarship when all of the ingredients in my mystery box stacked up to a posset! You can change up the fruit garnish if you can't get really ripe mangoes – something seasonal and at its peak of ripeness is ideal. Or you can skip the garnish and just have with a biscotti.

MAKES | 4

300ml (generous 1¼ cups) double cream

50g (1¾oz) caster (superfine) sugar

Zest of 1 large lime and 4 tbsp lime juice

1 ripe mango, diced finely

1 Put the cream and sugar in a small pan and bring to the boil. Let the mixture continue to boil, stirring thoroughly to ensure the sugar has fully dissolved. Remove from the heat and stir in the lime juice, mixing well.

2 Pour into 4 ramekins or little glasses and place in the fridge to set overnight.

3 Finish the posset by mixing the diced mango with the lime zest and serving on top.

parle-g chocolate tiffin

I think my affinity for Parle-G comes from their similarity to malted milk biscuits. The iconic little child smiling on the packet and their dinky little size makes for perfect tiffin-ing. An appropriately delicious treat for about 10 minutes of effort. If you can't get Parle-G, then you can use malted milk biscuits – or any other cookies you like.

MAKES | 8

40g (1½oz) golden syrup (corn syrup)

1 tbsp caster (superfine) sugar

160g (5¾oz) salted butter

50g (1¾oz) milk chocolate

140g (5oz) Parle-G or malted milk or other biscuits (cookies)

2 heaped tbsp 70% cocoa powder (without sugar), sifted

100g (3½oz) dark (plain) chocolate

Small handful of pistachios, chopped

1 Put the syrup, sugar, butter and milk chocolate in a saucepan and heat gently, stirring continuously, until everything has melted and is smooth and silky.

2 Break your biscuits (cookies) into the pan, add the cocoa powder and stir well.

3 Line a tin with cling film (plastic wrap) – I like to use a small loaf tin (loaf pan) or a brownie tray.

4 Press the mixture into the tin, making it as level as possible. Melt the dark chocolate and pour over the top, then sprinkle over the chopped pistachios.

5 Set in the fridge for a couple of hours or overnight.

6 Cut into little bars or cubes to serve.

index

glossary

achaar – pickle of vegetables and/or fruits

achar masala – Indian spice mix used to make pickles

ajwain seed – carom seed

aloo gobi – curry made with potatoes, cauliflower, spices and herbs

amchoor – dried mango powder

anardana – pomegranate powder

asafoetida (hing) –made from ferula, a thick root, which is dried and ground to create a spice

atta – chapati flour

baingan sabzi – spiced vegetable dish

besan – gram flour

bhature with chole – spicy chickpeas with fluffy, friend bread

bhindi – okra

biriyani – rice dish cooked with whole spices

borani banjan – Afghan aubergine (eggplant) curry

brinjal – aubergine

chaat – street foods, full flavoured and exciting

chaat masala – spice blend used on chaat

channa dhal – dhal made with split chickpeas

chapatti – flatbread

dalia –porridge

garam masala – popular South Asian spice blend

gulaab jammun – fried cardamom dumplings that are steeped in saffron and rose syrup. Often eaten at festivals.

idli – savoury rice cakes that are often eaten for breakfast

imli – tamarind

Indian green chillies – also called 'hari mirch' (hari meaning green and hari meaning chilli) – fresh, thin, finger chillies used in all sorts of dishes or eaten raw as a condiment

jaggery – unrefined natural sugar, comes in a block or ground

jalebi – deep fried sweet, soaked in syrup

kadai – fire pit

kalonji – nigella seeds

Kashmiri chilli powder – mild chilli powder

kasoori methi – dried fenugreek

keema – dish made of minced meat, tomatoes, chilli and spices

kheer – rice pudding

khichdi – dhal and rice dish

ladoo – classic round Indian sweet, often eaten at Diwali

malai – rich cream

masala dabba – spice tin

masoor – red split lentils

mathri – a buttery spiced flaky biscuit

meethi cheez – a little something sweet

mithai – South Asian sweets

naan – flatbread

pakoras – crispy battered fried items for snacking

panjiri – a snack made with wheat flour, sugar and ghee

papdi – crispy gram flour crackers used for chaat and snacking

paratha/parantha – buttery layered flatbread

Parle-g biscuits – popular Indian biscuit

pulao – rice dish

pyar – love, blessing

rajma – dish of red kidney beans in a sauce made from tomatoes, onions and spices

ras gulas – cream cheese balls in syrup

rasmalai – cream cheese discs in a thickened milk sauce

rotis, roomali roti – flatbreads

sabji – vegetables

sev – snack made from small and crunchy pieces of chickpea-flour noodles

shrikhand – sweet or dessert made from strained yoghurt

tandoor – clay oven

tarka – spices heated in oil or ghee

tarka beans – Indian baked beans!

tawa/tava – heavy frying pan for cooking flatbreads

tikkis – patties

toor dhal – dhal made with split yellow pigeon peas

uttapam/oothappam – South Indian rice flour pancake with toppings

NAMES FOR PEOPLE

biji (grandmother)

babaji (grandfather)

bibi (grandma or woman of the house)

mamiji (maternal aunt)

chachis, bibis and bhuas (aunties)

acknowledgements

For as long as I can remember, I have wanted to write a book and in August 2021, it became a reality and I am so lucky to have been able to share the initial news of this project with my Mother. In true Mrs Gidda style, we toasted with champagne, full of pride, love and emotion. We cooked together, we held on to each other and absorbed every moment of osmosis-like learning that was available. I think it is fair to say that this book arrived at a time when it was almost incomprehensible to create – but create we did, all under the watchful eye and inspiration of Sukey Gidda.

Mrs Gidda. From licking the spoon after making cakes to paranathas, to roast dinners, puddings and pakoras – it was at home where I fell in love with food. Initial kitchen disciplines, cleaning up as we cooked, tasting as we go – all taught at home rather than culinary school – stood me in good stead for the professional kitchen that neither of us knew I would eventually enter. Aside from practical skills and the ability to create utterly delicious food, my mother taught me that a sense of humour, being playful and having fun were the most important qualities to embrace in life and she is, of course, totally right. She has been my most loyal supporter, inspiration, rule breaker and my compass for making sure I am making the very most out of life. There really aren't enough words, my gratitude is eternal and I hope she is as proud of me as I am of her.

My Father, Hardeep. You allowed me the time, space and encouragement needed to create this book. I am so very grateful for all you have done for me, to enable me to keep on going to complete this. A special thanks for the endless prep you helped with: peeling, chopping, organising, making masala chai, cups of coffee, omelettes, and of course – being my my chief taster. You always said you were Mum's KP – but officially, and in print, I am so happy to promote you to Sous Chef! It has been incredible to share this journey with you, thank you for your support, your love, enthusiasm and your encouragement, I couldn't have done it without you. We did it!

Sanj, Davina and Amaira. Sanj you are forever asking me for recipes – here are 90 to keep you busy! There are a number of Mum's recipes and I can't wait for us to start sharing them with Amaira. You will of course be thrilled to see much custard, cauliflower cheese paranthas and the trifle we so love – but now there is no excuse to not cook for me! I hope this book will be something Amaira will one day use and she will be proud of. Badda wrote a book!

Holly Cowgill. You are the calmest person I have ever met. Food stylist extraordinaire, maker of amazing oat lattes and completely unflappable when delivering 18 dishes a day in peak summertime heat in a tiny kitchen. Thank you for your energy, your organisation, your playlists and your commitment to my first book – it has been an absolute joy to work with you. Thanks also to dream team Charlotte and Sadie who gave abundant energy and enthusiasm in the midst of a crazy week and heatwave.

Maria Bell. There aren't many photographers who will shoot 90 recipes in 5 days with a smile on their face and a sense of humour. Maria I salute you, and I thank you. Not just for your extraordinary talent, but your sensitivity, encouragement and celebration of this little cultural journey we embarked on together as we zipped around the country. Your interest and excitement throughout this project has been amazing and I can't wait to work with you again (with a lot less on the daily shoot list)! Huge thanks to Ariana Ruth who was instrumental in this huge week long undertaking of photography. I learned such a lot from working with you both!

Sarah Lavelle and the Quadrille/Hardie Grant Team, especially Kathryn Keeble and Claire Rochford in design. And the copy editor Stephanie Evans. Thank you for the opportunity to create something so meaningful and special to me. For working with me as this book evolved and for allowing me to celebrate not just my own story, but the eight other incredible women who feature within.

Sophie Allen, my editor. Travel companion, dining companion, sense checker, cheerleader and all round hero. Thank you for letting this book evolve. Thank you for your patience, your expertise and your genuine unwavering enthusiasm for South Asian food, culture and sisterhood. Special thanks for not judging my tendency to over-order anywhere we ate on this trip and for sharing so many wonderful stories of your own travels across India.

Family Majhu: Mamaji Malcom, Mamiji Gulshan, Ricky, Sandy, Sanjay, Iysha, Rav, Aria and Aman. A massive thank you for all you have done and all you continue to do for me, and for us. Thank you for being a part of this book, the journey, being on the esteemed tasting panel, and for your unwavering support and love. Mamiji – thank you for sharing your kheer recipe – and for being a part of this with me, it was so fun!

The remarkable kindred sisters within this book: Usha, Rajinder Auntiji, Chandini, Nisha, Mursal and Zorah Aunty, Ruchita, Lakshmi and Melissa and your families for welcoming me into your homes. Thank you for agreeing to be a part of this project. I wish we had more time and more pages as there was so much to talk about, so much to cook and so much to enjoy eating! Being invited to cook with you, learn from you and share with you has been so special. It is quite something to arrive as a perfect stranger and to leave as friends! I thank you for your hospitality, your kindness and for treating me as you would family. You will no doubt continue to inspire many, and in particular young South Asian Women. It is a proud moment to look up, look around and to see each other win.

Karan Sidhu, who kindly shared the opening photo of me and my mother. Taken at a wedding in India, it is one of my absolute favourites – and I am grateful to you, for capturing her magic, our relationship and much joy all in one shot. You are so talented and I hope one day we get to work together!

Theia, Anna and Team KBJ: Thank you for being with me through it all. It is just the beginning, but I love working with you and I look forward to all that is to come! Special thanks to you Theia – for being with me through the whole of this journey, you are amazing.

Jeremy and Family Ford, Samirah, Gaile and Lisa, Katherine and Lorna, Lale, Marcello and Kamil, Shenali, Kitty, Sarah, Rachel, Rebecca and Jane. Thank you for your incredible love, support and friendship, some over many many years. You have all been instrumental in keeping me going with unwavering love, generosity, kindness, wine and friendship. I am so lucky to have you. I love you all.

And of course, to everyone who has bought this book. I hope it brings you joy, that you feel a little like you travelled with me on the journey with it, that it made you laugh, that you enjoy cooking from it, stain the pages splashes, write in your own notes and share these recipes with those you love. Your support through buying this book means a great deal to me – and I just hope you adore it as much as I do!

Love Sabrina x

about the author

Sabrina Gidda's early career began in Fashion PR and marketing, before realising her passion lay in food and cooking. She has run numerous London restaurants along with overseeing the opening of members clubs both in the UK and US. She now runs her own consultancy, working globally with hotels, restaurants and brands to create food concepts and menu design.

Sabrina has enjoyed competing and judging in popular television shows, such as the BBC's Great British Menu, Celebrity Masterchef, Saturday Kitchen and Snack Masters. Her recipes have featured in *GQ Magazine*, *The Sunday Times* and she has crafted food experiences for Krug Champagne, BMW and Women for Women.

Sabrina is an Ambassador for Pancreatic Cancer UK, where she raises funds and awareness for a charity that is very close to her heart.

She wants this book to be a celebration of her Punjabi heritage, the Modern European cuisines she has cooked professionally and also her eclectic, inventive approach to food. She encourages you to cook great food with great friends and create great memories.

@sabrina_gidda

MANAGING DIRECTOR
Sarah Lavelle

PROJECT EDITOR
Sophie Allen

COPY EDITOR
Stephanie Evans

SENIOR DESIGNER
Katherine Keeble

PHOTOGRAPHER
Maria Bell

FOOD STYLISTS
Sabrina Gidda, Holly Cowgill

PROP STYLIST
Polly Webb-Wilson

HEAD OF PRODUCTION
Stephen Lang

SENIOR PRODUCTION CONTROLLER
Sabeena Atchia

Published in 2023 by Quadrille,
an imprint of Hardie Grant Publishing

Quadrille
52–54 Southwark Street
London SE1 1UN
quadrille.com

Cataloguing in Publication Data: a catalogue
record for this book is available from the
British Library.

Text © Sabrina Gidda 2023
Design © Quadrille 2023
Photography © Maria Bell 2023

ISBN 978 1 78713 912 1

Printed in China